BOAT BOY

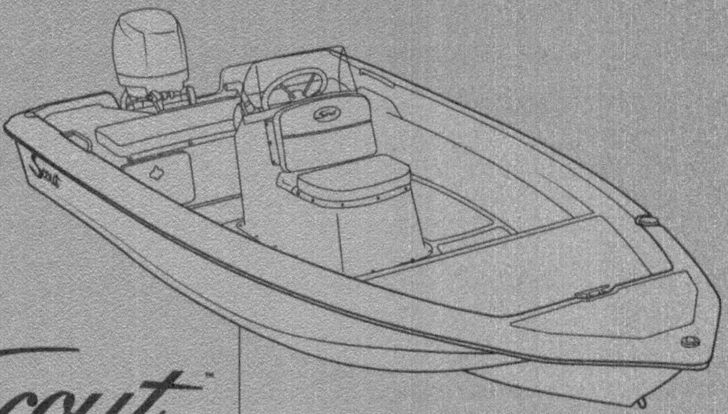

THE *Scout*™ STORY OF PASSION, PERSEVERANCE & PURPOSE

STEVE POTTS

BOAT BOY

Forbes | Books

Published by Forbes Books, Charleston, South Carolina.
An imprint of Advantage Media Group.

Printed in the United States of America.

10 9 8 7 6 5 4 3 2 1

ISBN: 979-8-88750-587-9 (Hardcover)
ISBN: 979-8-88750-588-6 (eBook)

Library of Congress Control Number: 2025901480

Cover design by Lance Buckley.
Layout design by Ruthie Wood.

03-19-2025 12:44

I would like to dedicate this book to my wife, Dianne, and to my son, Stevie, and to my two daughters, Sherrie and Stephanie.

My entire family stood by my side during the trying early years and continue to work for the company today.

CONTENTS

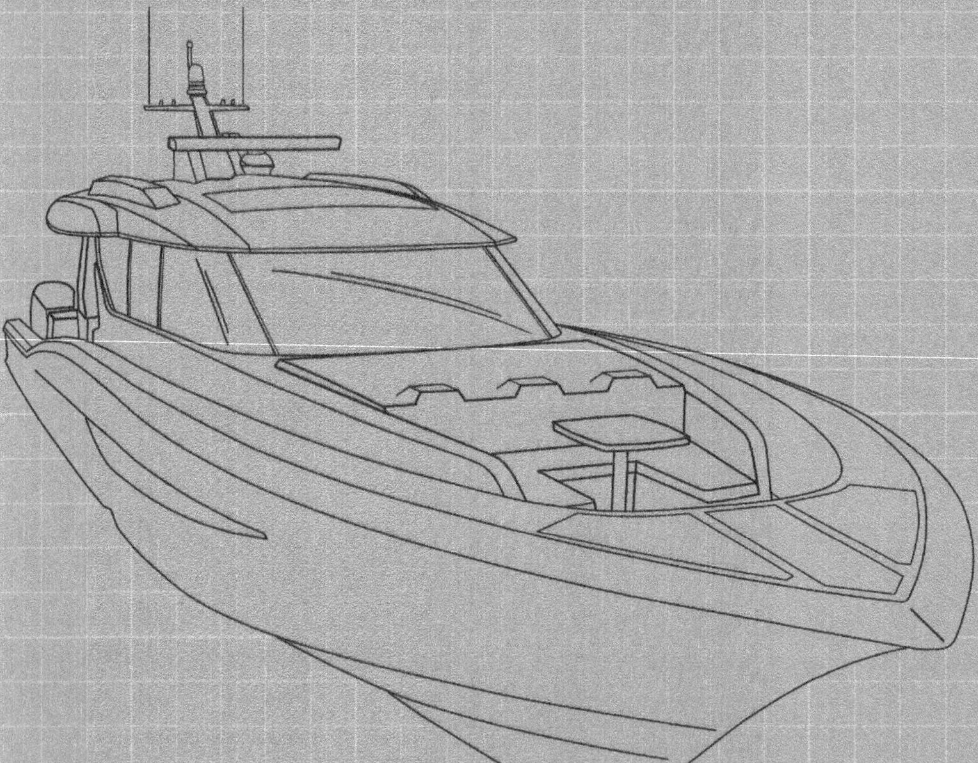

INTRODUCTION

The water is an emerald calm, lapping against our Scout Boat's fiberglass hull in some tributary dissecting the Charleston, South Carolina, archipelago. The sun shines all around us, the light speckled by an occasional puff of cloud. I'm fishing with an old neighbor, friend, and customer, Ed Marinaro, the former Cornell running back and Heisman Trophy runner-up in 1971, who played six years of pro ball and then embarked on a long and successful acting career. Many people know him as Joe Coffey, the Italian stallion police officer on the long-running TV drama *Hill Street Blues*.

Ed and I enjoy an easy friendship, full of the verbal banter common to guys, and especially to athletes, which only one of us was. Between sips of beer and false alarms at the end of a line, we tease and needle, our friendship like an old sofa you sink comfortably into. The only sound is us, the only agenda our shared tranquility, the peace one feels from fishing that can't be explained to those who haven't experienced the draw of the water. This is heaven on earth.

Fishing is a paradox: It's an escape into solitude and the joy of communing with nature, the cacophony of abject silence, the act of being totally present in the moment, and in a little hook cast into the vast ocean while the daily pressures of life drift away. At the same time, it's a unique bonding experience: two guys sharing this near-religious experience in the vast Atlantic with no other human within a thousand football fields.

Occasionally, we reel in a fish, or we don't; it doesn't much matter. That catch is thrilling but ultimately unimportant. As the existential comedian Steven Wright points out, there's a fine line between fishing and standing on the shore like an idiot. We aren't on shore, of course—I sell boats for a living—but there is something metaphysical about our activity that transcends the arrival of a sea creature.

"Hey, Boat Boy," he says.

"Yeah, Hollywood?" I respond.

This is a key element of the patter between us. I've spent my whole life building boats. He is recognized worldwide for his acting.

"Steve, I don't like being called Hollywood," he says. It makes sense, of course. Guy has an Ivy League education, a list of accomplishments on the gridiron that includes earning All-American status three times, a beautiful and talented wife and child, and a house on an island in Charleston, South Carolina. He moved out to LA to pursue acting but didn't like the scene as they say, which explains why he's now slumming with the likes of me. His success as a thespian is merely one aspect of his life, and reducing it to a stereotype can't be considered a compliment. I was never committed to the nickname, which could be bestowed on thousands of others anyway. It does not take much for me to discard it, but there is one condition.

"You know I don't like being called Boat Boy," I respond. Unlike Ed's relationship to Hollywood, my relationship with boats has endured my whole life, going back to my childhood. I began building boats as a kid, ran boat-making manufacturing operations for other companies while my peers were attending college, started my own company manufacturing and selling boats, innovated in the industry, and brought my wife and three children into the business along with their three spouses. Every penny I've ever earned in my life has been related to boats; most of the blessings in my life are related to boats; boats have steered into my path most of the people that mean so much to me; nearly every lesson I've ever learned and accomplishment I can claim begins with a hull and a deck, an aft and a stern, a port and a starboard. Boats even connected Ed and me.

And yet.

Boats have been the canvas for my life's art, not the art itself. Had I been excited by bicycles or houses or computers or anything else, I truly believe my trajectory would have been the same. The drivers of success are not the business one enters; they are the characteristics inherent to them that reduce the circumstances to mere details. Many of those who have achieved great success in business (and in athletics, as Ed can tell you) share the intrinsic qualities that drove us to build and grow Scout Boats into an admired and profitable company. They include vision, ambition, dogged persistence, optimism, and dedication to the craft. I also benefited from an inborn belief in other people's innate value and my desire to find the best in them, the unstinting support of my family, and a big, fat, healthy dose of luck. Anyone so endowed and so fortunate can start a company and succeed in whatever industry that, well, floats their boat.

Besides, "Boat Boy" suggests it was all inevitable—that I loved boats, so I created a boat-making enterprise, and people just naturally bought our boats. Build it and they will come. If it were only that simple. My wife, Dianne, and I had three kids when we began, one of them an infant. That first year, we invested our life's savings and all our time into creating a company. Our first try flopped. We kept at it, and just about the time we got our sea legs beneath us, a hurricane wiped out our uninsured operation. We could have quit multiple times; I could have returned to managing boatbuilding operations and made a good living. Dianne could have returned to her administrative position at a local hospital and enjoyed its high-quality benefits. But that's not what people like us do. We persevere because we have a vision, a determination, and a belief in ourselves; giving up and admitting defeat are not in our vocabulary. We couldn't let down our employees or abandon our vision. The following year we hit it big with our innovative designs at a big boat show in Atlanta, returning with hundreds of orders and the momentum we needed to build a $100 million company.

Being called Boat Boy feels like I'm being recognized for the cover rather than the book. It would be like calling Warren Buffett "Cherry Coke Boy," or Oprah Winfrey "Talk Show Girl." A literary friend told me there is a word for this: *synecdoche*. It's pronounced sin-eck-do-key, and it means describing something by one of its parts, like head of cattle or minds that control government. I don't want to be a synecdoche, and that's what Boat Boy feels like to me: just a part of who I am.

So Ed Marinaro and I now call each other Steve and Ed, and we are still neighbors and friends and still bond over a good day fishing. I know that Ed recognizes that I didn't just wake up one day, wave a magic wand, and build a successful company. My journey is a long and winding road, as almost any successful person's is.

My dad was a navy man, leading our family from one coastal area to another. I bounced from Connecticut to Lancaster, Pennsylvania (where I spent summers on my uncles' farms) to South Florida to the Charleston area in South Carolina, where we settled. Dad was deployed on submarines for six months at a time, so I was often left to my own devices, which was a tough row to hoe being a middle child and an introvert. I had a difficult time meeting people and making friends, but I did find an escape. Living in the Lowcountry, crisscrossed by bodies of water that drain into the ocean next door, I was always hearing the call of the water. On my way home from school every day during middle school, I passed a boatbuilding shop and was transfixed by the smell of the resin used in fiberglass. By thirteen I was working in the shop, and by fourteen I was helping to build these unsinkable fiberglass boats—one hundred of them in a year. The boats we built were known as Scouts.

While this was happening, I had the good fortune to meet people from various walks of life. From the rich White kids in Connecticut to Amish kids in Pennsylvania to oppressed Black kids in the South, one thing I understood intuitively, and had reinforced repeatedly, was that we were all, at our core, the same. Those surface differences never mattered much to me. I made friends wherever I could, regardless of our outward appearances or the prejudices others verbalized. This approach has served me well in a career in which I have managed many hundreds of employees and molded them into a cohesive whole dedicated to a single mission.

The middle school job led me to another and another as I climbed the managerial ladder in boatbuilding companies. I learned a lot along the way, mostly what not to do. I developed a credo predicated on employing best practices in manufacturing, treating employees like peers, striving for continuous excellence, and innovating relentlessly. I knew we could do something no one else was doing and fill a consumer need for reliable, top-end recreational boats at reasonable prices. With Dianne's navigation, I decided that I would establish my own company with that simple vision and began earning money with a side hustle to take the leap. Once we established that plan, we would not be deterred or denied.

While developing the plan, I attended a course at the Small Business Development Center with about two hundred other people. The director of the center informed us that only about forty of us would actually have the initiative to embark on the entrepreneurial journey. Of those forty, only eight to ten businesses would survive even a year. And of that handful, just three would make a profit and remain in business five years later. That stuck in my craw. I was determined to beat the odds, to rise above the crowd and demonstrate to the world—or at least myself—that I had a better idea and could bring it to fruition.

We were fully invested in our business. There were no bank loans, no rich benefactors, no investors—just the Potts family putting it all on the line. I had worked nights repairing the finish of damaged bathtubs to save the $50,000 that would float our operation until it could make a profit. That arrangement concentrated our effort because there was no fallback plan, no investors to return to for another infusion of cash. Husband and wife working six days a week, eleven hours a day with three kids at home was a challenge. With the help of a nanny and lots of intentional parenting, we juggled it all. I overflow with gratitude toward my wife, without whose support, participation, and confidence the company never would have launched. It's impossible to overstate how critical to the company's success she was, never faltering, never wavering in supporting my dream and my relentless pursuit of success. Then, in turn, the two of us relied heavily on a handful of outstanding employees to help us deliver on our vision.

Of course, long before we embarked on this journey, mentors and role models had helped pave the way, guide and shape me, and show me the right way to do things. Anyone who believes they made it on their own is delusional and narcissistic; I pride myself on being rational and humble. My two primary role models were Dick Fisher, the founder of Boston Whaler, and Dick Bertram, founder of Bertram Boats, two of the first and finest fiberglass boat makers in the world. I had many mentors, including Homer Norton and Jimmy Taylor at the Outboard Shop, which first employed me at age thirteen; Dave Stanton; who gave me my first management job as a nineteen-year-old high school dropout; and Jim Von Konon, who taught me how to create and measure manufacturing standards. There were many others, too numerous to name here. I stand on the shoulders of giants.

The first public unveiling of the yacht tenders we were building took place at the Newport Boat Show. A yacht tender is a small boat used to ferry passengers to and from a yacht. Newport, Rhode Island, is a swanky playground for the rich built on the yachting life, so it seemed natural for us to debut our creations there. We built all manner of displays and invested in a beautiful presentation for the sixteen boats we brought with us. We hoped to sell them all and take orders for more.

And then reality slapped us in the face.

Returning home with fifteen boats, no orders, and much of our money spent, we knew we had to steer in a new direction. That's when I remembered those Scout boats I had built as a younger man. I knew how to build Scouts to exacting specifications, efficiently. I knew how I wanted to value my employees, and I knew what customers were seeking in the high-end fiberglass market. Boston Whaler and Bertram made outstanding boats, but they didn't make fishing boats, and their models were expensive. So, we set about building 14- and 15-foot Scouts, lined up a half-dozen dealers in the Carolinas, and started over again. From that point on, we were turning a profit and preparing to grow. I was feeling my oats: My vision was coming to fruition and validating all the hard work and planning we had infused in the operation. But a fellow named Hugo had other ideas.

On the night of September 30, 1989, the winds of change crashed into our neck of the woods with a vengeance. Hugo, a category 5 hurricane with winds of 160 miles per hour, made US landfall a few miles inland of our plant in Summerville, South Carolina. It relocated a swath of the Atlantic Ocean into the South Carolina Lowcountry and obliterated any trees, cars, and buildings that had the misfortune of standing in its path—our shop included. Under mocking blue skies the next day, we returned to an uninsured structure best suited to a game of pick up sticks.

As we waited on the FEMA line for a $10,000 loan to buy groceries, Dianne expressed the only reservations about our enterprise she has ever uttered. Perhaps this was a sign from the universe that we should let the dream go and return to our comfortable lives, working normal hours, enjoying biweekly paychecks, helping our kids with their homework. It's the only moment of doubt she ever had, and it quickly passed. We felt our resolve was being tested and we could not fail.

Instead, we found a new site for our plant and began building boats one at a time, delivery check by delivery check, taking each payment to the bank to buy the next drum of resin, the next roll of fiberglass. That lasted all of two months until a freak pre-Christmas snowstorm buckled the ceiling of our building and soaked all our equipment, material, and floors. I felt like Job in the Old Testament, who was tested repeatedly but never relinquished his faith. But it wasn't just us. Everyone in the Charleston area was in the same boat, so to speak; we were not special in that regard. People were wondering where they were going to live; how they were going to get back to work, earn a paycheck, and buy Christmas presents for the kids; and just generally how they were going to rebuild their lives. The only thing we knew was that we couldn't give up. As Winston Churchill said, "If you're going through hell, keep going."[1]

Dianne and I had both enjoyed our success in the workplace, but we relished our independence, despite the trials and tribulations. The words of our trainer at the Small Business Development Center reverberated in my head, that only three of two hundred entrepreneur wannabes would demonstrate the resilience and acumen to flourish. In the wake of one storm after another—quite literal in our case—I was bound and determined to beat the odds. Perhaps more than anything, more than knowledge or genius or experience or capital, sheer dogged determination is the primary driver of success. Maybe we were naïve, maybe hard headed, maybe numb to reason, but whatever the case, we kept sailing our ship through the storms, seeking that red sky at night that portends sailor delight. As has been pointed out about Abraham Lincoln, he failed seven times in business and politics before winning the 1860 presidential election.

In the year of hand-to-mouth existence that suggested we were onto something, we began making our comeback. We were getting back on our feet, our staff was coalescing around the idea that we built the best fishing boats in the world, our designs were selling, and once again, we felt like we had turned a corner. In 1990, we decided to showcase our new Scout brand at a big boat show in Atlanta, where dealers from across the nation congregated to see the newest products

---

1 "Winston Churchill Quotes," Brainy Quote, https://www.brainyquote.com/quotes/winston_churchill_103788.

and innovations for their retail customers. We showed up with these three little boats, 14-, 15-, and 17-foot fishing vessels. We knew that our boats didn't look like anything else in the coastal fishing boat market. They were built different, and the fit and finish were superior to anything else. Remember Newport, where we returned with our tails between our legs, with no recourse but to go back to the drawing board? Just twenty months later, following a pair of business catastrophes, we walked away from Atlanta with two years' worth of orders despite an economy that was entering a recession. Between 1990 and 1991, we motored ahead at top speed, tripling in revenue, never to look back. Eat our wake, Hugo!

My vision for Scout Boats has never wavered. We build affordable luxury boats, like the Boston Whalers and Betram Boats I cut my teeth on decades ago. They are 100 percent handlaid, finely engineered, and beautifully finished, with innovative designs made for performance and reliability, all at a more affordable price than comparable high-end, mass-produced boats. You might think of us as the Acura of boats. With this as our North Star, our company has not just weathered the storms that could have sunk us, but thrived and earned a reputation for excellence.

Here are some independent testimonials that help establish Scout as a globally revered brand: BoatingSports.org says, "Scout boats are as strong, sturdy and reliable as they claim! These are good high-end boats that provide new dimensions in security off-shore!"[2] Boatingmag.com says, "The 530 LXF proved itself a magnificent craft."[3] Sportfishing.com says, "The 330 LXF is a first-class fishing machine enhanced by

2 "Are Scout Boats Good & Reliable Enough to Own?" BoatingSports.org, accessed December 17, 2024, https://www.boatingsports.org/scout-boats/.

3 John Tiger Jr., "Scout 530 LXF Boat Test," Boating, January 9, 2019, https://www.boatingmag.com/scout-530-lxf-boat-test/?srsltid=AfmBOoqkrSU6kW5jksUxm_LysfM9SqDxs3xvFo1pvQzIH3Bhcn-p6BfF.

luxurious appointments."[4] And BoatVirtue.com says, "Many boaters choose Scout Boats for their first boat, or as their forever boat because they know they can count on them to provide years of enjoyment out on the water."

Anyone who has built a company from the ground up or worked in a competitive field requiring constant efficiency and innovation understands that these results aren't inevitable; nor is continued success. They require daily recommitment to the core tenets that guide the enterprise from everyone involved—the CEO and the janitor alike. One of the few independent boat makers in the world, we maintain our maverick spirit, our quest for innovation, and our focus on delighting consumers, and that fills me with optimism about the future, even as I sail off into the sunset.

---

4 Jim Hendricks, "Scout 330 LXF Boat Review," Sport Fishing, February 27, 2020, https://www.sportfishingmag.com/story/boat-reviews/scout-330-lxf-boat-review/.

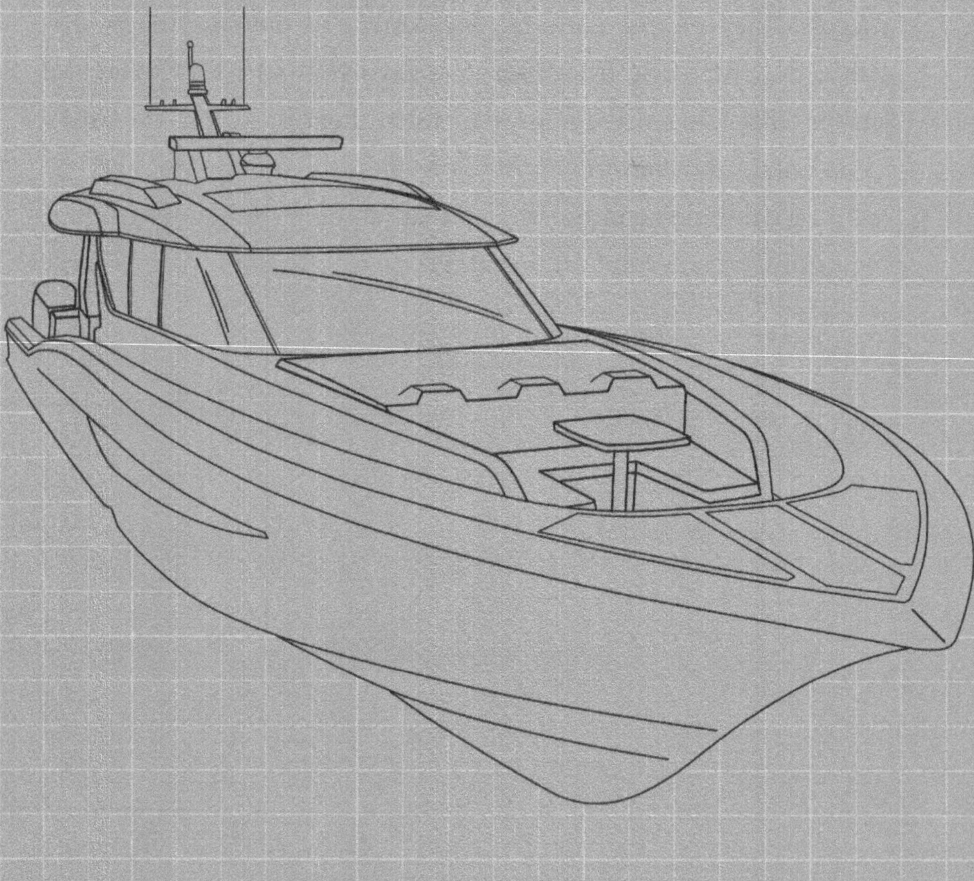

PROLOGUE

Being in the thick of a category 5 hurricane is like being in the throat of a screaming giant—a giant with endless breath that flattens trees and lifts cars, dropping tornadoes like fingers to scratch out splinter-littered paths where houses once stood. For endless hours you wonder if this is it, if your house will hold or if these are truly your last precious minutes on earth.

But then it stopped. Hurricane Hugo rolled dark and angry up the eastern coast, and we walked out of our home to find everything upended and unrecognizable. Our kids found a couple of sticks and started playing, the terror of the night before forgotten, and my wife held our nine-month-old daughter with a look of tired relief. It was a miracle we'd made it through. But in my heart, that fear was still there, hard and cold and certain that everything we'd poured our lives into for the past several months—saved for over the past several years—was gone.

There are times when I hate being right.

When the roads were cleared enough for local travel, we made our way to the old horse stable in Summerville, which had stood for more than a hundred years before we moved in with our small, two-person boatbuilding operation. The eye of Hugo had passed right over the little town, and as we rolled up, our fears were confirmed: The stable was nothing more than a pile of bricks and a few snapped oak beams. The promising start of Scout Boats was buried under that rubble, and not for the first time, I wondered if we were doing the right thing, putting our life savings on the line to follow a dream. But I've never been one to give up. And with the help of our nine- and twelve-year-old kids, we picked up those bricks, one by one, and recovered just enough to start again.

It wouldn't be the last storm we would face—literal or figurative. It wouldn't be the last time self-doubt would creep into our consciousness. And it wouldn't be the last time we would dust ourselves off and refuse to quit, even when a rational person might. The words of William Ernest Henley's iconic poem "Invictus" did not occur to us then, but we subscribed to the general idea: "In the fell clutch of circumstance, / I have not winced nor cried aloud. / Under the bludgeonings of chance, / My head is bloody, but unbowed."

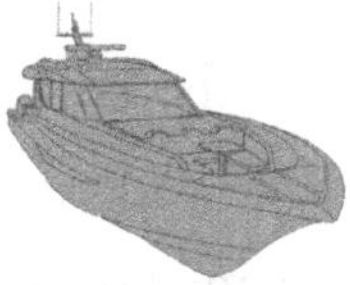

CHAPTER 1

Growing Up Along the Coast

Unfathomable realities of life intruded upon the little bubble I inhabited at the ripe old age of eight, when summertime fun meant climbing trees, fishing, picking beans, and playing boy games with my new best friend, Tyrone. It was the early 1960s in rural John's Island, South Carolina, to which we had just moved from New London, Connecticut, via Miami, Florida, at the behest of my dad's employer, the United States Navy. As a shy middle child, I was gleeful to make friends with a boy who shared my concept of fun, and we passed the months between school years exploiting the marvelous sea islands of the Lowcountry in which we lived. Tyrone lived in my development and was different from me in some notable ways that were irrelevant to us, such as his tightly curled hair, broad nose, and dark skin. In fact, all the kids in that development looked vaguely like Tyrone, except me, and that seemed fine with all of us. They introduced me to the game of half-rubber, a somewhat shocking derivative of baseball played with a broomstick and a rubber ball cut in half that zigzagged like a drunken fly.

In Tyrone, I found my perfect complement. I was shy and reserved, and he could talk 'til the cows came home. We'd bonded the first day we spent together and remained fused at the hip for much of the summer, which seemed to last for years because I grew so much emotionally at that young age. He introduced me to the famed "walking tree," this enormous Live Oak whose broad limbs reached so far from its base that they sagged to the ground under their own weight. It was so called because anyone could walk up to it, which is ironic today, since the five-hundred-year-old tree now known as Angel Oak is a prized natural phenomenon in the Charleston area. Its 28-foot-circumference trunk and 187-foot length are protected in perpetuity by the Lowcountry Land Trust so that it can never be dispatched to make way for condominiums or a Piggly Wiggly grocery store. More to the point, it is accessible only by paying a fee to enter the park around it.

But we didn't know any of that then, and I'm a bit chastened to mention that Tyrone and I carved our initials in the behemoth all those decades ago. I hope she recovered from our intrusion, and I hope Tyrone is happy and thriving today. We lost touch after that summer, but before we did, he involuntarily taught me an important lesson that has remained with me my entire life, so fundamental to my life's philosophy that I have passed it on to my children and grandchildren.

Tyrone loved Orange Crush, the orange-flavored Coca-Cola product that helped keep us from melting into a blob of protoplasm in the sweltering South Carolina summer. After my mother took me to the island's only 7-Eleven for an orange Slurpee, I was excited to regale Tyrone with tales of the transcendence of this icy treat, knowing that orange was his Kryptonite. Upon arrival at the self-same 7-Eleven in eager anticipation, armed as I was with the quarter that would unlock a frozen concoction for each of us, I noticed that Tyrone had tarried at the door.

"Come on, come on, come, on," I said. "This is where the ice is at."

"Stevie, I can't go in there," he replied.

"What do you mean?" I asked naively.

He pointed to the handmade sign on the door that said *Whites Only*. It was one of the oddest and, in retrospect, one of the most poignant moments of my life when the sad reality of segregation and discrimination hit me like a blast from Bull Connor's fire hose. Tyrone and I spent a summer without barriers, just affection, and we remained that way until school started and we went our separate ways, him to the Black public school and me to the White one.

I am happy to report that the cracks in segregation did show during this incident. When I asked for two Slurpees, the clerk behind the counter asked if one of them was for the boy left to kick rocks outside the store. When I admitted it was, he just grinned and filled the order. Hope mingled with sadness even in that terrible discovery.

It seemed obvious to me then, just as it does to most people today, that once you tear down the emotional barriers—whether it's the color of somebody's skin or the way they dress, the way they talk, who they love, or whatever—once you strip that away, a human being is a human being, and they have the same wants and likes and dislikes as any other. When I entered the job market and began junior high school, desegregation got underway amid consternation, fear, loathing, and a lot of regrettable anger and threats that brought out the police, turning our school into an armed camp. It was a sad time that I could never wrap my head around. It just seemed to me that we should all just live together and get on with being our authentic selves, though that language didn't exist at the time.

My experience playing with the Black kids in South Carolina and the Amish kids in Pennsylvania shared some interesting elements. In both cases, "my kind" made plain to me that consorting with "others" was frowned upon, to the point that, particularly with regard to race, I was judged and ostracized by the judgmental majority, adults included.

But I do believe that every event can be character building, and I gleaned from that perplexing experience that I would never allow surface differences to determine how I treated people. Instead, over the years, I have learned to dig deeper and understand people by how they respond to their environment, and I use those psychological insights to push the right emotional buttons to bring the best out of each individual I encounter, whether my children, my employees, or my friends. This mindset has helped me convince each of the five hundred employees at Scout Boats to engage with their work and share my commitment to excellence at the company, and to be proud to wear the name Scout Boats on their sleeves.

Here's an example of how that manifested itself in my career. At nineteen I was afforded the responsibility and authority to lead the finishing department at American Fiberglass, my first management job, with about twenty employees working under me. It was my job to teach them how to fix gel coat and all the other imperfections coming down the assembly line. All twenty were women, and just about all of them were old enough to be my mother. At the beginning, they manhandled me, undermining my authority, refusing to cooperate, and generally treating me like a snot-nosed adolescent, which wasn't far off the mark. I was taught to respect my elders and so felt constrained in my response; as a result, this insubordination went on for my first two or three months.

Finally, I decided to put my Tyrone epiphany to work on these women. Today we would say that I had developed a high EQ, but that language didn't exist in those days. I gathered them together and told them that though I was young, perhaps even young enough to be their son, I was not going to fail at this job, which could serve as the springboard to my career. I asked them to consider how they would want coworkers to treat their own sons and daughters who had earned their position because of their expertise in a particular area, regardless of their age.

That was the carrot. Then came the stick. I told them I refused to fail. I was going to succeed with or without each of them, that it was their choice. From that day forward, I said, questioning my authority or undermining my efforts would get them terminated on the spot. This yin-yang combination of appealing to their maternal sides and threatening their livelihood had the desired effect, for the most part, reestablishing my authority in the workplace. Still, 90 percent compliance is well short of 100 percent, which was my standard; the following week I fired two long-tenured employees who pressed the case against me. That got everyone's attention and transformed me in their eyes from the entitled juvenile they'd first perceived me as to a boss who was determined to help them succeed and was not to be trifled with. Over time, we bonded into a cohesive unit, and they came to realize that I was experienced and knowledgeable despite my youth. It also served as the workplace beta test of my theories on human psychology and my first opportunity to earn respect and demonstrate leadership in challenging circumstances. You might say it was my Dale Carnegie moment, though I hadn't at that point read any of his work.

But I've gotten ahead of myself. You see, by the age of nineteen, I'd already spent seven years in the boat business, five of them molding fiberglass and gluing it together with resin to create high-quality recreational boats. And even before that, the water had a hold on me thanks to a father who sailed the seven seas and returned home to a coastal city itching to get back on the creeks, streams, and rivers around Charleston with his son. When I was twelve or thirteen, we spent our summer weekends in these little 10-foot johnboats that he could rent from the navy for a few bucks, digging up oysters and running them back home.

It was at that time that I joined the juvenile delinquent club, though it was news to any adults at the time, and I waited a couple of decades before revealing it to my nonplussed father. A friend and I got it into our heads to build our own crude, flat-bottom, plywood boat using scavenged trimmings from the houses under construction in our neighborhood. This was before I could drive, of course, so I traipsed from site to site with a wagon and collected the detritus from the process—a couple of two-by-fours here, a handful of discarded nails there, and our self-applied elbow grease. At twelve, we thought we were pretty ingenious, particularly when we took the boat out into a local creek and it floated. We were doing better than the *SS Minnow* (or the *Titanic*, for that matter) right off the bat. But their fate was soon to be ours. It was my first lesson in understanding how important it was to pay attention to the structural integrity of the transom.

My father was out to sea again, and we wanted to do likewise, though unlike him and his fellow sailors, thwarting the evil Soviet Union was not on our agenda at the time. We simply wanted to go—and the faster the better. My dad had procured a used boat engine, and we decided that our flat-bottom boat would be a whole lot more utilitarian if it could take us somewhere rather than just float with the tide. We secured a couple of clamps and attached the motor to the boat, started it up, and gave it some gas.

Just in case you're not a sailor at heart and wouldn't know a transom from a transmitter, let me help you see the imbalance in this equation. Flat-bottom boats are the most hydrodynamic vessels possible because their entirety floats, displacing very little water. The more hydrodynamic a boat, the more swiftly and smoothly it can travel the waterways, just as an aerodynamic car can zip along at higher speeds on a race track. This is good! At the same time, our vessel is basically a little bathtub that weighs just a few pounds—however much a couple of dozen two-by-fours and some nails tip the scales. You see where I'm going with this, right? If you were to push this thing by hand across the water, it would skim lightly along the top with almost no resistance. Instead, we injected three or four horsepower at our boat's back. At this point, you should be picturing our wooden bathtub lifting off like the Wright Brothers' plane, and that is exactly what it would have done had it been more structurally sound. But we were twelve-year-olds with a hammer, not engineers in a manufacturing plant. That ten- or fifteen-pound motor was connected to a piece of wood at the back of the boat—the transom—and when the boat began to blast off, the piece of wood stayed home, weighed down by the offending engine. In other words, the transom splattered, dropping my dad's new engine into the creek.

You will be glad to know that the creek was just a few feet deep, so we fished the motor out of the water and spent several hours cleaning it of the approximately seven hundred pounds of pluff mud that had accumulated inside it. (This may be a slight exaggeration, but that's how it felt.) Pluff mud is the pungent, bacteria-rich, quicksand-like mud that makes its home in areas like South Carolina's sea islands, which are hot and swamp fed. It has the consistency of tomato paste and smells like rotten eggs. But we did a good enough job that when we returned the motor to my dad's garage, no one was the wiser.

Even better, this episode followed shortly after my mother had lent the motor to a family friend. When my father returned to shore duty and attempted to use the motor, it was the neighbor he quietly blamed for the plaintive sucking sound that emanated from it before the cylinders seized up, never to pump again. My dad had to throw that motor away, literally throw it in the garbage, a crime for which I offered my solemn admission of guilt and heartfelt regret after a cooling-off period of roughly twenty-five years. At that point, he was sufficiently convinced that I was an idiot that adding this minor episode to the supporting data was not going to change his opinion much. It was not until he saw Scout Boats become a thriving business employing hundreds of people that he started changing his mind, because there was a lot of evidence to the contrary earlier in my life to overcome.

But even this incident gets us ahead of ourselves. Even before the transom busting, the motor squelching, and my first experience with racism, there was my introduction to life in the South. Having lived in Connecticut and South Florida, and having passed summers on a Pennsylvania farm, I was unfamiliar with the rhythms and social hierarchy of life in the Deep South. This ignorance cost me an Indian burn and a verbal lashing, but again, taught me a lesson that guided the rest of my life. I learned this lesson at age nine in my first school days in South Carolina when I replied in the affirmative to my teacher's question. "Yeah," I said.

When I tell this story to South Carolina natives known as binyas (as opposed to transplants known as comeyas), they laugh uproariously at this point, aware of my shriek-inducing faux pas. And sure enough, my highly offended teacher grabbed me roughly by the arm, bent it in an unnatural position, and dragged me indignantly to the principal's office. Remember how we were all taught in grade school that this principal was spelled as it was because he was your pal? At that moment, the principal was my executioner. With the punishment paddle looming large and foreboding in the background, he offered me a withering tutorial in the Old South's social hierarchy, which required, among other things, that children address their elders, particularly elders in positions accorded respect like teachers, with *sir* and *ma'am*. Moreover, my days of "yeah" were to be immediately and permanently discontinued; did I understand?

"Yes sir."

Was I ever going to forget to address my teacher with respect?

"No sir."

How was I to indicate to my teacher a response in the affirmative or negative from here on in?

"Yes ma'am and no ma'am, sir."

Southern Manners 101 concluded, I was marched back to the classroom to apologize to my teacher and promise never to act so barbarian and ill mannered again, ma'am. Little nine-year-old Steve took the lesson to heart, and thereafter included in his vocabulary those two words in every interaction with an adult, a habit he passed on to his South Carolina-born-and-bred children and grandchildren.

That lesson in respect found itself challenged by the dissonant state of race relations I encountered in the next few years as a child, when Black adults were disrespected regularly by White children and adults alike. While I appreciated the focus on demonstrations of respect in Southern culture, this jarring exception bothered me, and I was glad to see the most overt forms of discrimination ebb away as I entered adulthood. It has always been my intention to find ways to connect with people and judge them for how they act, not for how the world says you should judge them.

My love of everything aquatic can be traced to my early childhood, situated across from mile marker 1 in Key West. Being repeatedly uprooted and changing schools presented social challenges for an introverted navy brat, but I could always count on the serenity of the water, crafting tiny islands of solace amid the chaos. For me, fishing and boating were the gateway to happiness. It was there I first discovered the joy of designing and constructing makeshift rafts and coarse boats from watertight drums and plywood, finding joy and peace on the soft ripples of the Intracoastal Waterway. Any friendships I could develop on that foundation were as solid as the ribbon of asphalt that formed the interstate. Thereafter, the hard work and play of farm life that had filled my soul for a couple of summers was replaced by a new heartthrob, and it was wet.

As I entered middle school, my homeward route took me past a garage where a mechanic was performing a special kind of magic—assembling small fishing boats made of fiberglass and welded with resin. The smell of liquid resin tickled my nose and my imagination as I lingered before him to witness the miracle of boatmaking every day on my way home. Boatmaking combined two innate thrills for me—the maritime and the mechanical. I've mentioned the lure of the water; I was equally hypnotized by building things. Under different life circumstances, I would have been an engineer. To think you could mold some simple materials with your own hands and fashion a craft that would speed across the water with them, that was exhilarating to me. The mechanic could see my fascination, and eventually he offered me a job cleaning up all the scraps for a daily fortune of twenty-five cents. It was at that moment that my interest in school, already a thin thread, completely unraveled in favor of a front-row seat to the art and craft of hand making this sophisticated machine. My affinity for cars, boats, and planes knew no bounds; had I passed an automobile plant daily during junior high school, I might have created the company building Teslas, but the title of this book is *Boat Boy*, not *Car Boy*.

The disposition of these handmade boats put the whole operation in the bonus round for me. The mechanic would take each one out to a gas station and peddle it to passersby, selling one at a time and making a profit. My preteen mind was attempting to wrap itself around the concept that you could spend evenings deep breathing that intoxicating resin, find fulfillment assembling this complex vehicle, and get someone to pay you for it. You could have the world's best hobby and make a living doing it. I don't know that I could articulate at that point much beyond loving hanging around the shop and being adjacent to the process, but there's no doubt that it was my gateway drug to the boatbuilding business, which even today still feeds my soul. And then, it got even better: I got fired.

With neighbors breathing down his neck about the stench from the resin, the mechanic decided he needed to discontinue the garage side hustle, putting me out of a job. For about a minute. He would concentrate on his full-time job as a mechanic in the Outboard Shop, where they built an upscale boat called a Scout, similarly handmade of fiberglass and resin. He suggested I swing by and apply for a job there, having learned the basics of boatbuilding at his side. Whatever small corner of my mind school was managing to occupy at that point gave way to an actual real-world job making money doing something I loved.

Let me take a small detour here and wax poetic about fiberglass. For centuries, boats were built with wood, and even at that time a lot of them still were. But wood rots, whereas fiberglass does not, and our big selling point about these little Scouts I began building was that they were almost completely fashioned in fiberglass, with the ironic exception of the transom, which was wood encapsulated with fiberglass. Even the seats were steel molds covered in fiberglass, so that the boat was unsinkable, allowing the Outboard Shop to offer lifetime warranties for its boats, quite the selling point when buyers were dropping tens of thousands of dollars on one.

From age fourteen to seventeen, I worked weekends and summers at the Outboard Shop making six times the minimum wage, then $1.25, eventually doing all the repair work and building the smaller Scouts.

Imagine how intoxicating this all was for a sixteen-year-old boy, earning more than some of the fathers in the neighborhood, learning a lifelong skill, and accumulating life lessons about how to work with people, how to run a shop, and so on. I could buy a cool car that would attract the ladies and fast boats to race on weekends, and between the money and status among my peers and the responsibility and maybe the resin fumes, school could not compete. With my father out at sea, I stopped attending class and instead began working full time during the day, while continuing to represent to my mother that I was in school. When she found out the truth, she went biblical, wailing and moaning, rending garments, and all that. Not literally, of course, but she was furious and asked some neighbors to intervene. It was pretty clear at that point that I was wasting my time learning about dangling participles and the Boer War when I could be building boats; I had been a poor student for a couple of years simply because my head was not in the game. But the owner of the Outboard Shop agreed with my mom, and so to mollify them, I took courses at the local community college to earn my GED and get some engineering credits while I pursued my boatbuilding career. And that lasted all of six months.

We started building race boats, and so naturally, I had to build and race them. It's not like I had a choice, being a red-blooded American boy with more money than he knew what to do with at age seventeen. Although the primary purpose of racing was purely recreational, I was learning some crucial lessons about boat performance—the running bottom characteristics that make them fast and stable—and I was testing that knowledge every weekend against my fellow racers. I put a big motor on a small boat and whipped up on the competition because I had a better understanding of its performance attributes than anyone else my age. Being a hotshot who could run a boat over 100 miles per hour was far more fascinating than solving equations about the force per unit of area in a solid, so school once again finished last in the race against everything else in my life. My parents were mortified; my father thought I was a dope, but I was self-reliant, mature, and respected by my peers and bosses for aptitude around boats, and my prospects were pointing upward, at least in the short term.

All that would come into play in the next great development—procuring my life partner. Like my business success, this involved several significant setbacks at the beginning but fortunately, because I was immune to reason, I persevered and won Dianne's hand. The thing is, winning boat races and driving a fancy red hot rod, well, I might as well have been the lead guitarist in a rock band. Though shy by nature, I had developed a certain level of confidence by age eighteen, and fate deposited me at the place all young men frequent when seeking the woman of their dreams: the Shoney's drive-thru. I was at the wheel of my GTO, and a comely small-town girl was in the passenger seat in the car ahead of me. So I pulled my car beside hers so that we were window to window, and, gentlemen, pay attention here because you are about to bear witness to a technique with the ladies that could change your life. We smiled at each other, and I bestowed upon her a pickup line for the ages, one that will undoubtedly be immortalized in the history books, placing me beside Romeo, Casanova, and Sir Walter Raleigh in the annals of suave purveyors of the craft.

"How tall are you?" I asked.

You see, I'm five feet six and was not inclined to date a girl who required me to stand on my toes to kiss. Being five feet five or shorter was a litmus test for all prospective girlfriends, and since we were both seated, I needed this crucial piece of information before commencing the full-on flirt. Some over the years, Dianne herself included, have mocked my opening salvo as awkward and unsophisticated, but I beg to differ. I was the model of efficiency, establishing a baseline for our relationship with four short words. Besides, scoff all you like, but the question elicited a laugh from her and began a conversation, during which three critical pieces of intelligence were gleaned: (1) She was five feet four, solidly in the Goldilocks zone; (2) She was a senior in high school, again, perfectly situated for my intentions; and (3) She had a boyfriend. This one was suboptimal.

Dianne had been dating a guy who'd joined the army, which inconveniently for them, had shipped him to Alaska—the very hour before. Dianne's world had been shattered, and she was drowning her tears in a burger and fries when I happened along in a hotshot car, prompting her troubles to melt away. Despite the possible complication of an incumbent boyfriend, I asked her out for Saturday, and we had a swell time on my boat, her meticulously coiffed hair blowing in the breeze like pelican wings. When I returned her to her house, there stood before us her brother and another fellow in a tux. It turned out that Dianne was headed with him to the prom that very night.

"Wait, I thought you had a boyfriend," I said, now finding myself dropping to third on Dianne's depth chart. But she explained that this guy was serving as her wingman for the prom in the absence of her one true love, now safely ensconced in the forty-ninth state. And, in fact, our relationship began to flourish over the next several months, and the boyfriend detail began to recede from my memory, until the fateful day she got in my car and said she had to tell me something. You know how nothing good ever comes from the girl you're dating having "to tell you something," particularly when there is this hazy recollection of a boyfriend? This was worse. It was a bombshell.

"I'm kind of engaged," she informed me.

The hits just kept on coming. I thought she had broken it off with Private Alaska, but apparently, from the looks of things, absence had made the heart grow fonder, and I was merely her way of passing the time until his return, which, I was informed, would occur tomorrow. In the meantime, he had mailed her an engagement ring with a letter professing his love and asking her to marry him. This may explain why Hurricane Hugo twenty years later did not deter me, because I had already endured an emotional hurricane as a nineteen-year-old with the girl I loved, the eye of that first storm passing directly over me, blowing my entire world off its moorings. Fortunately, the winds died down immediately when she told me that she hadn't accepted and that she was preparing to break the news to him the next day that she couldn't marry him, and in fact, unless he quickly procured a car hotter than a red GTO, the fastest boat in the Charleston area, and a job making several multiples of army pay, she was opting for the short guy with the stunning pickup line. That's not actually how she proposed to articulate it; I'm just rephrasing for clarity. A year or so later, we were married, and fifty years, three kids, several houses, and a thriving, respected business after that, I think I can say with some confidence that it worked out. But if Dianne ever decides she's done with me, I've still got a nice car, a good job, the fastest boat, and that amazing pickup line just ready to be coaxed out of retirement.

CHAPTER 2
"Why Don't You Just Build a Better Boat?"

When I was nineteen years old, with five years of boatbuilding under my adolescent belt, a gentleman named Dave Stanton called me up and proposed to offer me a job. "Who are you, again?" I asked. Among the millions of sentences I have uttered in my life, that might be the dumbest. Or at least the most laughable in retrospect.

Dave Stanton is, in fact, an icon in the boating industry. He was the manager of the Ithaca Guns plant in Belgium when he was hired by General Recreation to turn around their boatbuilding operation, called American Fiberglass, which built entry-level sailboats and fishing boats. He steered American Fiberglass to profitability and respect in the industry, then sailed off to establish his own company, American Sail. With over twenty-five thousand of the boats his company produced owned by sailors all over the world, it is one of the most successful sailboats ever designed and was inducted into the American Sailboat Hall of Fame in 2001. Dave himself chaired the National Sailing Industry Association for three terms and was awarded the industry leadership award by *Sail* magazine in 2002. Dave Stanton may not be on the Mount Rushmore of the sailboat business, but he's a first-ballot Hall of Famer. That is why requesting his bona fides was a bit like balking at taking a call from your state's governor because you don't recognize their name.

Dave wasn't all that quite yet, so my confusion didn't faze him a bit. I was working at the Outboard Shop building fiberglass boats, and Dave called to discuss a position at American Fiberglass. His sales pitch was, let's say unorthodox. He told me the company was in competition with AMF, a giant powerhouse recreation company that owns bowling alleys and built Harley-Davidson motorcycles for a while and manufactured boats of higher quality than American Fiberglass did. In fact, American Fiberglass was accelerating toward oblivion, Dave told me, because of its 110 employees, not a single one knew how to build a boat correctly, and that was the environment he was proposing I should join. He had been recruited to turn this enterprise around, and he had heard that I could help him accomplish that. To sweeten the deal, he offered me significantly less money than I was earning at the shop. How could I refuse?

I was working six days a week in the finishing department, counting my money, driving my hot car, racing fast boats, and impressing short women at night and on my one day off, but I agreed to go to the company's warehouse and meet this guy with the screwball offer. The improbability of this rendezvous escaped me at the time, having had no frame of reference for the career arc of ordinary people, but I hadn't even graduated from high school, and here I was getting recruited for a managerial position I hadn't sought.

Dave explained to me that he wanted me to join the finishing department and train the staff how to finish a boat correctly. A finishing department is basically quality control at a boatbuilding operation. It is a group of people that fixes all the chips and cracks and imperfections in the boat to prepare it for sale. The irony of this proposal was that I had never seen a finishing department before because we built our little Scouts at the Outboard Shop the right way the first time, and so we didn't need a whole department to patch our mistakes and touch up our poor craftsmanship. It was my good fortune that I had been taught how to build a boat—or anything, for that matter—the right way. My early exposure to recreational boats had been with two of the finest brands in the world. Boston Whaler and Bertram were like the Rolls-Royce and Mercedes-Benz of boat brands, where imperfections were not tolerated and only perfection and excellence were accepted. I had no idea that my obsession with fit and finish, my dedication to exactitude in the gap around the hatch, and my overall commitment to superior quality were outliers in the industry. A testament to my naiveté, it was all I knew. Later in life I established a side hustle repairing boats and encountered lesser-quality brands that struck me as pieces of junk. I was flummoxed that anyone spending all that money on a boat would opt to buy such shabbily constructed vehicles.

My one and only experience with imperfection in a boat I had built came a couple of years earlier, by which time I was already flexing my muscles about my ability to construct a high-quality Scout boat. It's a real challenge to stay humble when you're in eleventh grade with classmates who don't know how to screw in a light bulb and have never earned a penny in the working world while you're outearning some of their parents constructing seaworthy vehicles that consumers purchase and enjoy. I mostly kept my hubris in check, but it squeaked out one day on the floor of the Outboard Shop to the detriment of a cockroach that had ambled onto the fiberglass hull I was assembling. (Sorry, palmetto bug. The way we avoid having cockroaches in South Carolina is by bestowing upon them a different name.) I was spraying the gel coat on the mold when I spotted the palmetto bug and zapped the sucker with the gel, fossilizing him for posterity and dispatching him or her to eternity on the seven seas. It's not the worst fate, if you ask me. Anyway, we finished that boat and sold it, and that was that. For a while.

Some months later, owners Homer Norton and Jimmy Taylor came to me and asked me to take care of a customer whose little Scout emergency-backup boat had a bug in it. It hadn't yet occurred to me at that moment that they were being literal because the guys were always picking on me, being the youngest staff member by nearly a decade. I went out and looked at it, and the man who owned the boat was standing there, and Mr. Taylor was standing there, and Mr. Norton was standing there, and they pointed their fingers at the side of the boat where the gel coat was flaking off, and Cocky Cockroach—if you're going to have a pet you should name him—was pinned to the side of the hull, not interfering one iota in the proper function of the vehicle. I immediately confessed my sin to the assembled and begged forgiveness, but they were too busy getting a good belly laugh at my expense. I brought the Scout to my work area and cleaned it up, so the hull was as smooth as a baby's bottom. We all agreed that the boat was good as new, and everyone lived happily ever after. I mean, the cockroach wasn't having much fun, seeing as how his time at sea had come to an end, but he didn't complain much either, so we all considered that his silent acquiescence and went on our merry way.

The point is, that was the closest I had gotten to being satisfied with anything approaching poor quality work, which left me unprepared for the concept that Dave Stanton was presenting me: namely, that a factory of 110 people turned out such low-grade products that a whole department was necessary to undo all their lousy craftsmanship. Perplexed, I asked him, "Why don't you just build a better boat?"

"Precisely," he replied, and escorted me to the finishing department, where nineteen people labored every day to fix or cover up the carelessness of their coworkers. No one in the finishing department complained about the substandard quality because it was that very thing that kept them employed. As the great investor Charlie Munger once said, "Show me the incentives, and I'll show you the outcome." The outcomes at American Fiberglass at that moment were second-rate boats shoddily assembled, as I was about to witness firsthand.

Dave showed me a boat that had come off the line with a hundred holes in the cubby cabinet that slept two people. I asked him why they were putting holes in the boat, and he explained, in a level of detail that would cure your insomnia but fascinated me, that they were being lazy and reckless and that this problem was endemic to the operation. He wanted me to be a problem solver and trainer—to teach these people how to correctly build and finish a boat—and for my time and expertise, he offered me the princely sum of twenty or thirty dollars less per week than I was already making.

When I protested, Dave dealt me the first of many lessons I would learn from him. He said, "Son, let me give you a lesson in life and in careers. When you reach the top of your capabilities in a certain market, which is where you are now, where are you going to be in ten years?" There's the ladder of being a laborer, and there's a ladder of being a manager, and you sometimes have to go from the top of the laborers' ladder to the bottom of the managers' ladder.

Perhaps if I had been more mature, I would have pointed out politely to Dave that while I appreciated the long-term value of changing jobs, he had called me, he had a disaster on his hands and he needed me to fix it, and he could just as easily start me at the same salary I was making at the time. Earning a manager's wage was not mutually exclusive with moving up the managerial ladder. But I was nineteen, and he had me hook, line, and sinker. Showing off the hot car and fast boat had paid off now that Dianne and I were getting serious, and I was beginning to think about my future and the opportunities that lay before me. I knew that while I was precocious in the boatbuilding department, all I had to do was stay there for a few more years, and I would just be another high school dropout laborer. I wanted to earn more money, not less, but I had a clear vision of how taking this management position could catapult my long-term prospects to greater heights. Besides, when someone courts you and sings your praises and offers to fling open the door to your future, it takes more moxie than an insecure teenager has to push back. And that is how I found myself manhandled by a gaggle of indignant women, presenting me with one of the inflection points of my very nascent career.

As I've mentioned, these twenty women ran me ragged for about three months, undermining my authority, openly disdaining my training, and refusing my orders. While I respected their elder status and long tenure relative to mine, I also knew what I could not say to them, which was that I was imbued with a level of training and knowledge about boatbuilding that had thus far eluded them and that they could learn a lot from me despite my youth. I understood that no one wants to take orders from someone half their age, but when that person is significantly more expert in the activities in question and is working to rescue a failing business to which you owe your employment, one would think that maturity would convey some humility. This is another of those sayings that we didn't have then, but I was asking them to trust the process and draw their conclusions only after the outcomes were apparent. Unfortunately, none of them subscribed to this theory, at least not in the first ninety or so days. Indeed, they openly mocked my requests and carried on with the same dysfunctional activities as before. We were not making much progress.

The salient fact about boatbuilding is that it is a labor-intensive process that requires every single person who touches the boat to value fine craftsmanship and employ the mindset of a perfectionist. There is no boatbuilding machine or boat assembly line; the final product is as finely crafted as the least-skilled person in the process can create. Consequently, it only took one or two contrarians to ruin both the process and the quality of the boats we were building—or in our case, finishing.

The women of the finishing department displayed two miscalculations: (1) They underestimated my relentlessness, and (2) They failed to recognize the Golden Rule—he who has the gold makes the rules. My one ace in the hole was that Dave had hired me to succeed at turning around the performance of the finishing department and was married to my success. He was going to support me in those efforts. Emboldened by that knowledge and my own ambition, I took the action described in chapter 1, announcing to the crew that I would accomplish what I'd been hired to do, either with their help or without their employment, and when I terminated two recalcitrant women with long histories at the factory, I earned the attention and grudging respect of the remainder. Both women politely dismissed took their cases over my head, but management had my back and escorted them out the door. Thus did a punk-sized, teenage, high school dropout professionalize a twenty-member department of experienced middle-aged women. But I would be glib if I made it sound as if it was easy or a moment to relish.

I found it emotionally and psychologically draining to spar with women whom I felt I should be respecting and to whom I should be deferring. Their termination followed a long string of issues and constituted an absolute last straw, because I understood that I was affecting another family's livelihood. I lost a lot of sleep worrying about the hardship I might be visiting upon their families but also knew that tolerating their subordination would undermine my authority and the team's ability to improve and grow in skilled craftspeople. As Casey Stengel, the manager of the New York Yankees during their championship runs in the '50s, observed, his primary job was to keep the two guys in the dugout who hated him away from the twenty-three who hadn't made up their minds. I didn't want these two women to infect the rest of the crew. Fortunately, the two women who failed to heed my repeated warnings about workplace comportment were secondary sources of income in their households, which explained their behavior and alleviated some of my anxiety about their involuntary departures.

People who hear my story regularly ask me how I came about my maturity at such a young age, particularly without any formal schooling beyond eleventh grade and really, beyond about eighth grade, because once boatbuilding made its entrance on the stage of my life, school exited stage left. At several junctures in my formative years, I went weeks without attending school until my mother or employer discovered it and demanded that I at least make a token appearance and effort to pass. Molding and gluing fiberglass into waterproof transportation always fascinated me in a way that social studies and trigonometry did not.

The best answer I can muster may be found in the accumulation of hills I was obliged to climb to find my path in life. As the shy middle son of a navy submariner who was off to sea six months a year and whose family frequently changed hometowns, I faced many challenges coming of age during the turbulent civil rights movement. Passionate about cars and boats but struggling to fit in, I was forced to exit my comfort zone and clear my own path.

Moving forced me to make friends anew at every stop. Being the middle child between a privileged older sister and coddled younger brother forced me to develop an independent streak. It all conspired to teach me a handful of life lessons that have served me to this day. One was how important it was to treat people the same no matter who they were or what station they occupied in life. Another was to recognize each person as a unique individual and determine the method and tone of communication that achieved the best results with them. And the third, in the immortal words of basketball coach Jim Valvano on the eve of his death: "Don't give up; don't ever give up."

Those three life lessons have carried me past, around, over, and through debilitating failure to ultimate success, and Dianne and I have passed them down to our children and expect to do the same to our grandchildren. Studies of accomplished business leaders have demonstrated that success depends more heavily on persistence than on graduating from an Ivy League school or expertise in a field or truly anything else. I had just gotten married at the time and was more determined to succeed than to have everyone like me, though I am a people pleaser too.

That is not to say that I did this by myself, quite the contrary. There is no such thing as a self-made man or woman, because everyone who crosses one's path may teach some lesson, even a negative one, or affect life's trajectory. I had parents and friends and a wife and coworkers and bosses who paved the way to my transcendent career arc, one well beyond my wildest dreams.

I count Dave Stanton as one of my principal mentors despite our many differences in temperament and outlook. Dave was a very astute businessman who was hired repeatedly to turn operations around, which often meant bad news for incumbent managers and employees. Dave had a reputation as a hatchet man who would observe a business for a couple of weeks, determine the weakest links, call a staff meeting, climb up to the mezzanine deck, and terminate seventeen people at once. Then he'd turn to the rest of the staff and indicate that he'd better have gotten their attention because he was about to outline the steps to be taken to improve operations and save a sinking ship. Dave was a tough dude who brooked no unprofessionalism. He brought an unwavering focus on continuous improvement and a toolbox of measuring sticks to gauge progress along the way. I communed for many hours with Dave's time studies and performance standards, often called key performance indicators (KPIs) today. Dave liked me because, like him, I believe in doing what I say I'm going to do and tolerating no excuses. In my view and his, there is a time for fun, and that time must follow, not precede, the achievement of goals. I like to think that I have fewer rough edges in going about it, but that doesn't detract from my lifelong respect and appreciation for Dave and all he taught me about the business.

Early in my tenure at American Fiberglass I learned an important, if embarrassing lesson from our chief engineer, Jim Von Konon. Jim taught me the ins and outs of creating standards and quality control procedures, and how to measure our performance against those standards. He had us fill out these simple little efficiency reports every week that required a little arithmetic, which I'll risk curing your insomnia by relating to you, so you can see how the reports worked and why they caused me such trouble. If math causes you to break out in hives, skip the next paragraph and rejoin the discussion on the other side of it.

In Jim's rubric, the time it took to accomplish every task could be projected and standardized. If a task should consume 1.8 hours but required your team 3.6 hours to finish, you're operating at 50 percent of maximum efficiency. The goal was to get as close to 100 percent as possible, though realistically that would be impossible to maintain because of the human factor. Standards don't shoot the breeze about last night's episode of *The Sopranos* or take a bathroom break. I had no problem with this calculation, having taken some college engineering courses while studying for my GED, neither of which I finished, thanks to the call of boatbuilding and racing that I couldn't help following. I managed to ratchet up the finishing department's efficiency rating from 70 percent to about 83 percent, the best rate of all the departments, and was feeling pretty good about myself at the first supervisors' meeting that Jim convened. I was expecting hosannahs from Jim, maybe a big raise, a promotion, and even a parade in my honor. Things were looking pretty sweet when he opened my report, read it, wadded it into a ball and threw it at me, hitting me in the chest. Then he chewed me out for failing to write in the narrative section below why we hadn't made 100 percent. He told me never to turn in such a poor excuse for a report again and went on like that for long enough to indicate that this was a big deal to him. I was shocked and mortified; I could feel my face heating up and turning burnt sienna.

After my humiliation in front of the other supervisors, Jim pulled me aside and reassured me. He said he saw promise in me and didn't want me to get complacent or self-satisfied. He knew he had upset me, but he wanted to get my attention. The narrative section was the learning section, he said, the part of the report that required me to think about the barriers to perfection and how we might surmount them. If you have three new hires who aren't yet up to speed, or two of your key staff were out sick, or whatever, you have to explain that and consider how you might address these issues in the future, for example, by improving the training of new hires and cross-training staff to fill in when workers inevitably become ill. I was a proud young man who believed in doing things the right way, so I took that lesson to heart. Thereafter, I wrote the most comprehensive reports filled with every detail I could dredge up because I wanted to show Jim I could write the best narrative ever! As you can imagine, I never earned another reproach like that again, but if I had, it would have been for writing ridiculously overwrought narrative that wasted Jim's time. Fortunately, he recognized the lesson had been internalized, and he left well enough alone. It is not my style to humiliate people—I believe that you praise people in public and criticize them in private—but I can't argue with the results in that case. That lesson has stayed with me my whole life.

I spent six months whipping the finishing department into shape, pushing our performance higher and higher, gaining confidence and the respect of my department and other coworkers. By age twenty I was promoted from trainer to supervisor of another department, where I focused on learning something every day about how to succeed in business and how to convince people that they want to do what I wanted them to do. Above all, I hoped to educate and inspire people to be great at their jobs and be part of something they could take pride in. I like to say that throughout my career I've learned a lot more about what not to do in manufacturing than about what to do. I've learned a lot more from my mistakes and the mistakes of others than I ever have from our accomplishments. Two of the things I'm most adamant about not doing are neglecting to deliver on promises and accepting failure. Once I can convince an employee that those two items are sacrosanct, we tend to get along fine.

It is worth mentioning that none of my friends in those early days understood my drive and my total dedication to boatbuilding. It is a sickness with me, even today, sitting on a 42-foot fishing boat with all the first-class amenities, my entire mindset is dedicated to how I might improve its performance or its lines or its fit and finish. During my teens and early twenties, when my friends were going out and having fun, attending college, and experimenting with adulthood, I was working with the throttle pinned to the console, driving forward in my career at 100 knots, totally devoted to the work and its attendant benefits, like money and nice things.

By age twenty-five, now with a wife and child and eleven years of boatbuilding under my belt, I was named plant manager at American Fiberglass, a leader of 130 people, most of whom were older than I was. I had reached what many would say was the pinnacle of my profession, or if not quite the peak, at least the base camp, where many are satisfied to stop and fashion a stellar career doing something they love in a position of authority, making a good living, and creating quality products. No doubt, that was my mindset, for the time being. Once again, my life was ruled by performance standards, time studies, and efficiency ratings, the stuff we today call Six Sigma, continuous quality improvement (CQI), etc., and once again I was determined to blow everyone out of the water with the best results we'd ever had.

Ha! Shakespeare noted that "the course of true love never did run smooth," and since boatbuilding was one of my two true loves (my bride of fifty years being the other), I discovered that fate had different plans for me and my entire team. Having turned American Fiberglass around, Dave Stanton could see that he had created a saleable asset and split for calmer waters, while I found myself, along with the entire AF team, set adrift as the company's owners cashed in and sold to an outfit from Connecticut. The company, which knew bupkes about boatbuilding, at least knew to bring me and my brother-in-law, Fred, up to the Nutmeg State to effect the merger and build a new operation.

I knew this was not a permanent solution, so while I headed up to the Northeast for ten days of every two weeks, Dianne and the kids remained behind in Charleston, to minimize the disruption in our lives. Before Fred and I could set our plans in motion, we were informed that part of the company's business plan was to employ staff through the government's CETA program. The 1973 Comprehensive Employment and Training Act was a federal law designed to train low-income and long-term unemployed individuals by subsidizing their employment in the marketplace. The idea was—and remains, though the program has experienced numerous incarnations and names—to provide chronically unemployed people an opportunity to learn on the job and enter the workforce. This public-private, market-based partnership has long had bipartisan support, and were I running a convenience store, or carpet manufacturing plant, or other labor-intensive operation that required relatively low-level skills to succeed, I would have gladly helmed this group. But as Steve and I explained to the company, boatbuilding requires craftspeople fully invested in the quality of their work. Most of the forty-seven CETA workers we inherited didn't speak English, exacerbating the challenge, and while the company continued to believe that boatbuilding merely involved a series of tasks requiring x hours of labor for each task, we found ourselves chasing our tails until we wore a hole in the floor into which the entire operation spiraled. After two years, the bank took ownership of the company's assets and hired us to identify what those were and how much they were worth. In short, Fred and I spent two years rolling our eyes at the boneheads commanding our ship until it finally ran aground, leaving the chronically unemployed back on unemployment and the two of us to pick through the pieces.

A Rhode Island firm bought the company for a song with a plan to resurrect it, absent the CETA workers this time, with Fred and me serving as consultants. I bided my time for a year, and then Dave Stanton came to my rescue again, this time hiring me to help him run the boatbuilding division for American Sail. This is the point at which I had my epiphany.

Here I was, taking orders from someone else again, employed by my fourth company in two years. Though it was a good gig and I was earning a boatload of money because my compensation included a percentage of the profit based on efficiency, I had learned just about everything possible not to do in the industry. I felt that this job running another boatbuilding division for someone else was going to serve as the springboard to the establishment of my own company. After six or seven years of earning a nice salary and spending all of it on my growing family, our big house, and nice cars, I realized that the only way to transform a dream into reality was to commit to it. Launching our own company was a promise that Dianne and I made to ourselves, and you know, I always do what I say I'm going to do.

In order to execute our plan, we first needed some start-up scratch. I established a separate company to take jobs at night fixing fiberglass chips and scratches on whatever large boats I could find and bathtubs in the Ferguson warehouse down the road. There was plenty of work at the number one plumbing supply company in the US, and even more when another plumbing company hired me for more of the same. At this point, I was running a boatbuilding plant by day, fixing tubs at night for twenty-five to thirty-five dollars per unit, and coaching kids' soccer on the weekends. At that rate, I needed to repair two hundred tubs to reach my goal, so I had my work cut out for me. I may have slept intermittently in 1987 and 1988, but I don't recall when. In those two years, I salted away the $50,000 that Dianne and I had agreed was the minimum necessary to launch our new enterprise and sketched out the plans for our first boats. With the help of a second mortgage, the two of us quit our lucrative jobs, hired on an employee, and embarked on the adventure of a lifetime.

We could not have known then the gut-wrenching lows or delirious highs we would experience, the thousands of hours we would dedicate, or the unbelievable reputation we would develop with Scout Boats. What we have built, more than any boat, is a living entity that provides a livelihood to five hundred families and will outlast Dianne and me, carried on by our children and their spouses, and we fervently hope, their children and grandchildren and so on for generations to come. But I've gotten just a bit ahead of myself, because first we needed to go through hell and back.

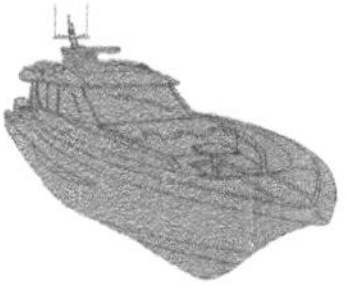

CHAPTER 3

Keelhauled

It was late 1988, and I'd reached my goal to sock away $50,000 and scratch that entrepreneurial itch. We had two young kids and a third child on the way, and we had good jobs making a very comfortable living. Now we were abandoning all that for the high-risk entry into a new boatbuilding business, one that would end the cycle of working for others, making money for them, and operating according to their rules, which we knew weren't always optimal.

It is difficult to capture our feelings at that time because I spent so little effort to catalog or understand them. Dianne and I were hell-bent on securing warehouse space, purchasing raw materials, pinching every penny, and arranging childcare for our brood while we worked long days and nights. With the help of one employee, the three of us were a lean, mean fighting machine, focused on our one goal of building quality boats. We knew that would only carry us for so long before we had to start selling product and bringing in revenue, but for the time being, we were singularly focused on the reality on the ground and not on squishy feelings. With hindsight, I can now identify the swirl of emotions that catapulted us through this whirlwind. With all our savings and then some on the line, we were anxious and scared but also excited and confident. I knew that I could build great boats—reliable, high-quality vehicles like Bertram and Boston Whaler—but more affordably. I had a track record of designing finely tuned watercrafts and of leading and managing a team. There was no doubt in my mind, nor in Dianne's, that we would succeed, but I was hazy on what success meant. Little flecks of uncertainty did manage to seep in the cracks of my mind, gnawing at my subconscious, feeding my determination to build a profitable company and show everyone I had ever worked for that they were doing it wrong.

Much has been made of Tom Brady, generally recognized as the greatest NFL quarterback of all time, leveraging doubts about his ability and his modest draft status as motivation throughout his career. Drafted in the sixth round by the New England Patriots, the 199th player to be selected in 2000, Brady was widely viewed as slow and unathletic, a backup in the league at best. Even after his seventh Super Bowl victory at the age of forty-three, when his then-wife asked him plaintively in front of millions of people, "What more do you have to prove?" he continued to nurture that indignation, seemingly sacrificing his marriage to return yet again to the gridiron rather than commit himself full time to his family. If a superstar athlete earning tens of millions of dollars could find motivation from a slight twenty years earlier, certainly I could leverage a bit of pride to sell some boats.

My situation was not nearly as dramatic, nor have I earned the equivalent of seven Super Bowl victories and multiple Most Valuable Player awards, but the need to prove something to someone, even if only to oneself, provides vigorous incentive to fight through the setbacks and achieve success in any endeavor. I'll leave it to the armchair psychologists to determine the source of my motivation: Was it proving something to my father, who thought I was a dope for dropping out of school, for pursuing boatbuilding, and for diving heedlessly into my own high-risk venture? Or am I seeking the posthumous approval of my mother, who felt deep regret about my lack of interest in education? Or am I attempting to prove mastery to myself, a short, shy middle child who has always needed the big car, fast boat, and nice house to signal my financial success? Did I need to prove myself worthy of Dianne, who was originally dazzled by my façade—the hot car and fast boats (and world-class pickup line)? Or is it something else buried so deep in my subconscious that I can't even dredge it up even as I dedicate real brainpower to the subject?

The unquestionably correct answer is "I don't know," and I've never invested the time and brainpower to explore. Also likely correct is "yes"—it's probably a little bit of all of those, and something more as well. Whatever it is, I have this disease, and it has spurred me to a lucrative and fulfilling career, and more importantly, to a life that is all I could have imagined and more. Dianne and I have truly been blessed beyond our wildest dreams, not only by the success of our company, the financial resources it has provided us, the famous people we get to meet and exotic places we are privileged to visit, but also by the more deeply satisfying opportunities it has provided, like the ability to mentor hundreds of people including our children about business and life and to see them grow and prosper as a result.

I do know that two major lessons stayed with me from a course I attended at the Small Business Development Center prior to launching my business that also lit a fire under me, one because I heeded it and the other because I did not. The first lesson was to diversify your investment capital at the start: Invest your own money for one-third of the upfront capital, secure a bank loan for another third, and obtain the final third from some outside investors. Investing your own hard-earned money gives confidence to investors that you have skin in the game and will work like a demon not to fail. Earning a loan gives your operation credibility and extends your bankroll to start. Investors provide access not only to capital but to experts, business acumen, and connections in your industry, the community, or elsewhere, depending upon your need. We ignored this advice, bootstrapping the entire operation, confident that I knew the industry sufficiently, could capitalize the operation adequately with the money we had and a lot of shoe leather, and uninterested in sharing the profits that we were convinced we would soon earn. Putting it down on paper might make us sound like arrogant and reckless boneheads, but I had twenty years' experience and felt I'd been equipped for this stage of my journey, particularly given the steadfast support and teamwork from my wife. We could always borrow money or bring in investors later, but we had good reason to believe that we could bankroll the whole operation ourselves at the start.

The other lesson undergirding our unstinting pursuit of success came from a statistic offered to the two hundred attendees of the conference. As mentioned in the prologue, the director of the Small Business Development Center informed the room that only eight to ten of us would survive a year in business and just three of two hundred would turn a profit and remain in business five years later. That shocked me, but also fired me up, as if he was throwing down the gauntlet and issuing a personal challenge, telling me the score was 197–3 against me. I was going to show him, them, the world!

Even as I internalized this challenge, I knew that my business was unlike most of the others in a variety of ways that boosted my odds of success. I was entering an industry that I understood top to bottom, one that had proven its appeal to customers. I knew the dealerships; the vendors of the fiberglass, resin, and other raw products; the landmines and battlegrounds; and all the competition's strengths and weaknesses. As a boat owner myself, I could relate to the people I hoped would be the customers for my product. And maybe most advantageous of all, I did not have a backup plan. In addition to all the other motivators, sheer desperation might be the most powerful. I had spent two decades working for other people, learning the business bottom to top, but also executing their poorly devised plans, employing their cockamamie processes, building the wrong boats for the wrong customers according to their demands, and participating in their misinterpretation of where the market was headed. Returning to that—to the life I had scrimped and saved, toiled at night, mortgaged my house to leave—was simply not an option. Based on all that, not to mention a thick skull that refused to process overwhelming odds, I dragged my family into this tornado, confident that we would not only emerge unscathed but vastly improved.

During my final months at American Sail, I worked at home building wooden molds for the yacht tenders we were going to sell. These were sleek, nostalgic vehicles with teak combing and seats that were designed to service yachts, stored in a utility shed in my backyard and covered with tarps while Dianne and I were off to our day jobs. That way, we would hit the water running on day one, with designs ready to produce and no costs yet borne. It was heartening that both of our employers—the hospital and Dave Stanton—tried to talk us out of leaving, but we were committed to chasing our dream, no matter how daunting.

And so it was that we rented an old brick horse stable in Summerville, South Carolina, about thirty miles north of Charleston, where Dianne and I labored long, grinding hours without pay to meticulously construct each handcrafted boat near as possible to godly perfection. Despite the gaping yaw of uncertainty before us, those very first days were thrilling because our one job was to build the boats of our choosing, our way, according to our plans and our designs. And for the moment, nothing else.

It's been said before that it's not what you don't know that hurts you; it's what you think you know but don't. I naively calculated that $50,000 was a lot of money with which to start a business. Sure, if you're opening a nail salon or putting out a shingle for marriage counseling. But less so for a manufacturing entity. We can hardly build three boats of our smallest Scout model today for that price, but back then, when we kicked off the company as Sail Pro—my initials, SP—we squeezed every penny so hard it made President Lincoln cry. The problem we faced was as old as capitalism: economies of scale. While large manufacturing operations can order supplies in bulk at nice discounts, we were ordering just enough to build the next yacht tender and paying the highest rates. But with few other expenses and a barge full of determination, we built and sold one unit at a time, squeezing out enough profit to buy the next roll of fiberglass and batch of resin and recoup a Benjamin here and there from the pile of cash we were burning through. What's more, it was 1989, and we were headed into a recession—a short one it turned out, really just a blip in the long march upward from 1983 to 2006, but we didn't know that then. There were many voices advising us to wait until the economic storm blew over, but we fervently believed, and believe today, that establishing a company during a downturn is advantageous, because if you weather the storm and make a name for yourself with consumers, you are positioned for logarithmic success once the skies clear for brisker business. At least that's what I tell myself now. More likely, the timing was right for us, marketplace be damned. As anyone with kids knows, when you've gotta go, you've gotta go.

I'm still proud of the tenders we built then. They were classy and reliable, and their progeny live on today among the offerings at Scout

Boats. But as we were about to find out, they were not the apple of everyone's eye at that time and place. As in comedy, business success is all about timing, and timing is largely an external force outside of your control. It's said that many great leaders would not have been so recognized had they come along at a different time. Martin Luther King Jr. brought the force of moral persuasion to a nation clamoring for civil rights. Bill Gates and Paul Allen nerded out on computers at just the moment when the world needed geeks to create the software revolution. Sail Pro unveiled the most gorgeous yacht tenders you ever did see, just as the boating public was turning its attention to fishing and recreational boats, producing a giant yawn unheard around the world. It was the worst thing that could have happened to us, and of course, the best.

We saddled up sixteen of those yacht tenders and trailered them north for their great unveiling at the annual Newport Boat Show in Newport, Rhode Island, summer home of the rich and gilded, dotted with eight-figure mansions and more wealth than a Berkshire Hathaway annual meeting. If you can't sell yacht-attendant products in Newport, you can't sell them anywhere. We paid a king's ransom for a spot in the show, and I hand-constructed glittering display units designed to present the dazzling tenders, about which we oozed with pride, in the very best light. This was to be our launching point for success, where we expected to sell the sixteen samples and take orders for many more. Our coming out party was set for the rocky Atlantic shores, where our destiny would be realized in America's smallest state. Though nerve wracking, it was an exhilarating moment.

And a quiet one. We spent the entire show emulating the Maytag repairman: unneeded, unnoticed, unappreciated. We sold one boat. We wrote no orders. The sonic boom of uninterest reverberated in our ears for four days as we atrophied in our booth, lonely as the new kid in school on his first day. We hauled the other fifteen tenders home, our tails between our legs, our dreams shattered, our souls crushed, each of us stewing silently in our juices. It's sixteen hours of driving from Newport to Charleston's northern suburbs, sixteen hours of staring forlornly into a windshield and wondering how it all went so terribly wrong. Sixteen hours of wondering what we could have done differently and how we could possibly move forward from this crushing defeat. But one can only stew about failure for so long before attention inevitably turns to how it can be made right. We built beautiful boats that no one wanted, but what if we built beautiful boats that people did want? What if we reincarnated the old Scouts that had served as my gateway drug to boating, streamlined throwback boats that many boaters wished they could own but couldn't afford? And what if we made them the right way, hand hewn, employing the most efficient processes I had learned to master during my twenty years in the business and sold them at prices that would entice more consumers? As the dotted lines added up beneath our wheels and the miles dragged on through New England, the Northeast, the mid-Atlantic, and eventually down South, my depression turned to determination, and my determination hardened and then transformed into exhilaration.

Through the pall that had fallen over us, I was glimpsing the real future of our company, soon to be rechristened with the name of the boats that had been lost, until then, to history. I could see through the haze of defeat the wisps of victory, the inflection point that would alter our direction onto the path to prosperity. By the time we arrived in Summerville, I was one night's sleep away from turning the company around. Of course, with the blitzkrieg of ideas coursing through my brain, there was to be no sleep that night.

It was heartening right from the start to have Dianne 100 percent on board with my pivot plan. She knew what those Scouts had meant to my past and understood intuitively how they could transform our future. We got right to work designing and building Scouts, my new vision taking shape in wood, then fiberglass and resin. We rechristened the company Scout Boats and began building little 14- and 15-foot fishing boats—sleek, nostalgic puppies, priced for an upscale but not necessarily rich fisherman to afford. During the week I was gluing fiberglass together, and on weekends I was dragging a trailer up and down the East Coast offering dealerships a piece of our new vision. The response from most dealers was warily positive—they liked the concept but weren't generally prepared to commit during a recession. But we did sign on some dealers and started writing an order here and there. It was grueling work, but it was small bits of validation for our notion that you could build great boats at reasonable prices. It was the spring and summer of 1989, and the tide was turning our way.

Note to self: When everything's coming your way … you're in the wrong lane.

One dealer visit that stuck in my mind, not to mention my craw, occurred in St. Augustine, Florida, another historic city among the first settled by Europeans and still a tourist mecca for those interested in early American history. I decided to call on the top dealer in the area who specialized in little boats like mine, a perfect target for my salesmanship. Arriving on a hot July Saturday, I immediately saw the parking lot stuffed to the gills, the joint jumping with potential buyers and the salespeople running from one prospect to another like fire ants pouring out of their mound. I approached a young guy who turned out to be the owner's son and showed him my Scouts, whereupon his face lit up and his body vibrated as if the Holy Spirit itself had invaded his body. He was ecstatic about our boats and told me his dealership could sell a pile of them. I was grinning from ear to ear when he ran off to retrieve his father, the owner of the dealership, but that grin began to fade as I waited ten minutes, fifteen minutes, twenty minutes before the boss finally appeared. And he was pissed. He started reaming me out in a whirlwind of four-letter words, including some new ones I would have to research later. He poked me in the chest and demanded to know how I had the nerve to come calling when he was busy.

I began apologizing and backpedaling because I sensed the next communication was going to be five closed fingers. He belittled me in front of his staff and a dealership full of customers, running me off in a fog of recrimination. I never forgot the way he humiliated me, and a year later, when we were introduced at a show and he expressed interest in selling our boats, I reminded him of the revolting scene he had acted out at his dealership and told him he would never have the privilege of partnering with Scout Boats. And thirty-six years later, that dealership still cannot sell you our products, much to their detriment.

The summer of 1989 was an encouraging time, as orders grew, our vision became increasingly vindicated, and the chastening of the Newport show receded in our memory. Spirits were high, but there was violence in the air, and its name was Hugo.

Folks here on the South Carolina coast say earthquakes and tornadoes sneak up on you, but hurricanes muscle up over distant waters, spinning their threads of angry wind into hot yarns, carving their way through the Atlantic and giving us plenty of time to scatter before crashing on shore. We even have a name for our getaways—*hurrications*. Living as far inland as we did, we'd never before run from a hurricane, so we stayed put and watched in shock and horror as Hugo roared directly through our neighborhood as a category 5, dropping Niagaras of water from above and rumbling up our street, sounding like a litter of wounded cats. We had never experienced a tempest anything like this one, whose eye passed right over us and raged for many terrible hours across the land the last week in September, unleashing destruction beyond us, through the South Carolina midlands and charging into central North Carolina, flattening buildings, snapping pines and live oaks, and pushing torrents of water fifteen feet high. Hugo remained a tropical storm well into the Great Lakes and inflicted $11 billion of damage along its path, including to our little uninsured horse barn and all its contents, forty miles from landfall. All that remained of Scout Boats were the hands that had built them and a game of pick up sticks. In the aftermath, my small children actually played an informal version of that game, collecting slivers of our erstwhile warehouse and attempting to identify them. It was their grim effort to turn catastrophe into child's play.

As we stood gratefully in the FEMA lines for the $10,000 handouts we all received to cover necessities for the next few months (thank you, fellow Americans, for being there when we needed you!), my mind swirled with the thoughts of our triumphant return, like a boxer chastened by loss but confident in the rematch. We had established a profitable operation and, Hugo notwithstanding, were feeling buoyant and confident. The business was viable: We were selling a product people seemed to want at a price they seemed to think was fair. We had banked some cash that was going to finance our revival, so Hugo was a tremendous blow, but not a fatal one, and I remained optimistic about the future despite this giant step back. Recovering from Hugo was a massive undertaking physically and logistically, but it did nothing to dampen our long-term confidence in our journey. The destination merely got pushed a little further away, as if the ill winds had blown it down the road along with our roof. I believed anything else was the express train to failure, and I was steamrolling my way to success, no matter how long it took.

We got quickly back on our feet and decided to focus our attention on another show, this one at the World Congress Center in Atlanta in November 1990. I know what you're thinking—are you nuts? Wasn't the Newport show a crushing blow, one that literally caused the demise of the company? Weren't you in a vulnerable place in the immediate aftermath of Hugo? Yes to all of that, but we also knew the timing was right. We felt more prepared for Atlanta than we were for Newport, even though we were starting physically from scratch. We had proof of concept and were ready to get our boats before a larger audience and let them see that a fishing boat didn't have to be purely utilitarian; it could be comfortable and beautiful as well. We knew we had something innovative and believed it would spark interest with dealers at the show. It led us to harbor visions of orders falling like snow from the sky.

Snow did fall from the sky that Christmas, shockingly for Charleston, South Carolina, actual frozen water crystals, cold, wet, and devastating. Three short months into the region's initial attempts at recovery from Hugo, a freak blizzard dumped eight inches of snow on our area, our largest snow total in recorded weather history. As a point of reference, we had witnessed less than one inch of snow in the entire decade before that. In a state that owned all of three snow plows—and none within two hundred miles of us—it was another catastrophe in a series that would bring out a sardonic smile from Mr. Murphy and his iconic law. The accumulated weight of the thick, water-laden snow caved in our workshop roof, which was not designed to carry a wintry load, damaging the boats we had just begun building and drenching our supplies, ruining many of them.

By now we'd faced enough pummeling to buckle the boldest spirit, and indeed, it prompted the first and only sliver of doubt in Dianne, who thought perhaps the universe was trying to tell us something, and not subtly either. Who could blame her? The Newport-Hugo-snowstorm disaster spree had barely covered six months, a drumbeat of setbacks that rarely would have augured well for the long-term prospects of any business. But I was so determined that I convinced myself that bad news comes in threes and that the blizzard had completed our trifecta; calm seas would follow, for sure. Besides, the narrative in my head had a happy ending that interfered with my ability to accept defeat. The gauntlet thrown down about failing businesses at the Small Business Development Center continued to motivate me: I was not going to let even a crushing string of defeats interfere with the script that played out in my head. We were going to be the 2004 Red Sox, who used a bloody sock and a well-timed stolen base to overcome the same 3–0 deficit to the hated Yankees and charge on to their first World Series championship in eighty-six years. Bloodied but unbowed, I recharged Dianne's spirits with my undaunted determination, and together we reentered the fray. Atlanta loomed just ten months ahead, and we were not to be denied. We were nothing if not scrappy.

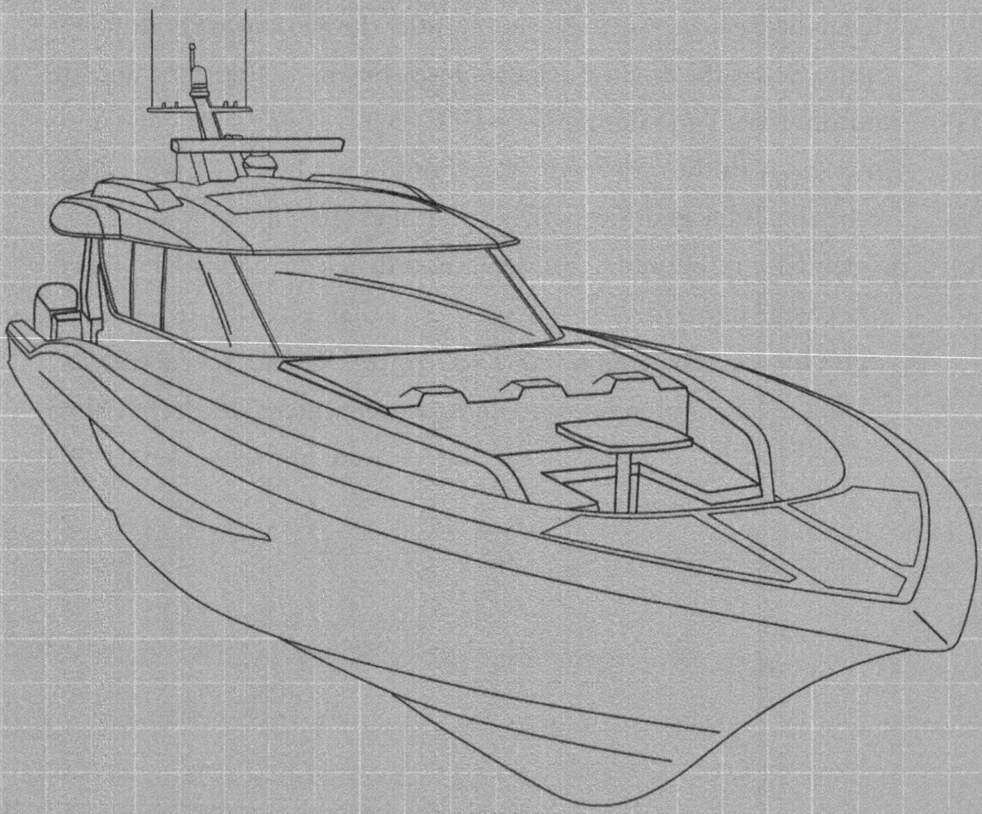

CHAPTER 4
A Barn Burner

Up until our foray into the industry, fishing boats were purely functional, much the way trucks were. People wore hip waders in them and spilled blood and guts on the decks, and they disdained anything that prized form over function. The boats were cramped and unadorned, designed for an exclusive tribe of manly men doing manly things, asserting their dominion over creatures of the sea—and maybe an ice-cold adult beverage. But just as truck manufacturers began transforming their vehicles for sale to soccer moms by enlarging their cabs, adding CD players, and installing carpeting in the passenger compartments, we offered a renaissance of creature comforts and sold to customers beyond the hardcore fisherman. We believed that families would take our boats out for a spin—sure, maybe to do a little fishing but also to swim, sunbathe, and engage in other activities—and then motor over to a restaurant dock for dinner. We had demonstrated to ourselves that there was a revolution brewing in the industry, and we were on the cutting edge of it, ready to launch.

I've always been a student of branding and could see the market shifting to the lifestyle we were selling—family time on a fishing boat rather than dudes out alone or in small groups for a day of hardcore fishing. I've always admired great brands like Mercedes and Harley-Davidson that sell more than just their product but the lifestyle they represent. Harley-Davidson, the bad-boy bike for outsiders and rule breakers, had taken it on the chin from Japanese manufacturers selling higher quality motorcycles to Americans who just wanted to enjoy the freedom and adventure of the road. Teetering twice on the brink of bankruptcy in the 1970s and '80s, its new owners realized they needed to tell the story of their riders. They upgraded their quality and shed their outlaw image while continuing to market the bike for rebels and rebel wannabes, establishing a tribe of Harley owners who ride together, gather at Harley "rallies," and earn tokens for riding. Harley owners purchase branded gear and prefer the tuning of the Harley engine, which runs louder than other brands. Today, Harley has rebounded to global icon status because its bikes are merely the centerpiece of a community that even an accountant can join. Whole doctoral theses in marketing have been written about the Harley brand shift and the resulting company rebound from bankruptcy to 160,000 bikes sold annually worldwide. This shift was analogous to the shift we were introducing to the boating industry, in that we proposed to improve the quality of fishing boats and make the lifestyle accessible to the wife and the kids as well.

The idea was an homage to the little Scouts I began building at age fourteen and cut my teeth on through age eighteen. The fit and finish were superior to that of the crude fishing boats of the day. Everything was polished, even the bilges. We took the philosophy of Boston Whaler and Bertram without all the cost, which felt to us like a winning formula. I had met Dick Bertram and Boston Whaler's Dick Fisher as a teenager and marveled at the awe they inspired and the respect they engendered for the unstinting quality of their creations.

I believed the boating industry still admired those qualities and they could be imported into fishing boats.

In addition to our relentless resolve going into Atlanta, we had Fred. Fred Withrock was a veteran of the boating industry, my mentor and advisor, who served as our sales rep and guide for the Atlanta show, then called the American Marine Trade Expo. Wholesale shows aimed at selling to dealers are different than any retail boat show you've likely attended, which would have targeted individual buyers. These dealer shows, of which that was one of the last, are forums for boat makers to introduce their newest models to dealers, gauge their interest, establish or enrich relationships, and take orders for future shipment. At a retail show, the culture of the show is largely irrelevant because most attendees are not part of the culture. But dealer shows have their own cadence and unwritten rules to which manufacturers and dealers adhere, and for that we needed someone with a deep understanding of its rhythms.

Fred helped us navigate the nuances, connected us with dealers, and dramatically boosted our odds of success. We paid him a premium for every boat we sold and order we took, so Fred had as much riding on the Atlanta show as we did. In fact, he introduced me to the North Florida dealer who had coarsely reamed me out the year before. Fred was mortified when I informed the dealer that we would not allow him to sell our boats. That cost Fred a pretty penny and, horrified by my emotional outburst and the loss of a potentially lucrative sale, he admonished me not to let my emotions interfere with business, something on which I had prided myself throughout my career. But the dealer's actions had been beyond the pale, and I would not relent. Fortunately, things worked out for Fred, as you're about to see.

We had built slightly larger boats this time—17-footers with a few more amenities and a higher price tag that we believed the market could absorb. Loading up the trailer with the boats felt like the worst kind of déjà vu, but whereas we had been rudderless in Newport, we now believed we were steaming full speed ahead to market prescience in Atlanta.

Our company was two years old at this point, and we had already been visited by three of the ten plagues—a convention crash and burn, destruction by hurricane, and destruction by caved-in roof. Locusts and slaying of the firstborn remained on the table, but we were a tight operation, with three young kids at home and a PhD in adversity. And we had one more heart-stopping moment ahead of us. You see, that 17-footer did not magically appear by rubbing a lamp: I had to design the prototype, which I finished—at 11:00 p.m. the evening before we headed to Atlanta. Once again, failure was staring us in the face, this time of my own doing, so that besides my near-panic state, you could add regret and self-recrimination. The 172SF was ready to go just in time. But that wasn't the end of the problem.

In my haste to finish the boat, I had neglected to take into account the need to move it out of the barn in which we were working. Whoops. You don't have to major in physics to know that an eight-foot, four-inch-wide boat can't get through a barn with an eight-foot opening. Imagine the scene: It's pushing midnight the night before the show five hours from home that will make or break us. And we can't get the brand-spanking-new prototype on which our dreams rest out the door. The sweat was pouring down my neck, the frustration swelling up inside me, and the embarrassment reddening my face. But I'm an engineer at my core and a problem solver by temperament, so I removed the spikes from the gigantic barn-door frame and with great effort dragged the door to the side to remove this shiny new model to load it onto the trailer. A week later we could all share a good laugh over this last-minute snafu, but at the time it felt like it might just be the nail in the coffin of our company.

I honestly don't know what would have become of the company had we fallen flat on our faces in Atlanta, but I'm happy to say our faces remain undamaged. Facing do-or-die stakes, we worked feverishly against the clock to finish the 17-footer for that pivotal show. Following our long travails, we invested our blood, toil, tears, and sweat, not to mention every penny we had left, to claim victory there. With our last dime, we were in sudden death overtime—win or go home.

Being ahead of your time is a prescription for failure if the time you were made for doesn't materialize for decades or centuries. Consider Vincent van Gogh's art or Charles Babbage's 1822 computer or Leonardo da Vinci's parachute. None of them earned a dime (or guilder or lira) for their creations because their work was unrecognized in their day. Being in the space we believed we occupied was different. The marketplace was poised to shift our way; indeed, it had already offered hints that the shift had begun. Boat manufacturers hadn't come to grips with this shift, but the dealers had begun to. After all, if you want to get the pulse of the market as it turns, talk to the people who interact with consumers every day—the retailers. Some within the industry were perplexed by our approach and advised us to attempt something less unconventional. When you're a trendsetter, you're doing something that hasn't been done before by definition, and not everyone will understand that it's something better. Fortunately, we were wise enough not to listen to the naysayers. We listened to Fred, and to the early stirrings of the marketplace.

We entered the Atlanta show in November 1990 with six dealers selling our boats and a World Congress Center permeated by doom and gloom as the recession began bearing down on the American economy. Boat dealers were skittish and pessimistic entering the show, and we had to make a special effort to avoid their contagion. We showed up with these three little boats, a 14-, 15-, and 17-foot scallop, none of which looked like anything else at the show. Unlike Newport, where even the crickets avoided us, we were met early on with curiosity from dealers. Clearly what we were offering—top-quality fiberglass fishing boats with sporty styling, plush amenities, and lifetime guarantees—was a departure from not just the ordinary but the perceived wisdom of the day.

Zig when everyone else is zagging, said Warren Buffett, and we took his advice, though we could hardly have identified him or that quote at the time. Just as clearly, dealers had an inkling that the boating public was itching for the boats we were proposing they purchase. In fact, some of the dealers, many of whom were boat owners themselves, identified with their customers' mindset, conflicted about taking their families out in their fishing boats because they were such lowbrow affairs, not conducive to family time on the water. Their curiosity grew into interest, interest into excitement, and thank goodness for Fred, who translated excitement into orders. And then more orders. And then more orders than we had ever received before. By show's end, we had signed on more dealers asking to show more boats than we had ever sold in the entire history of our company. We set the show on fire, sold all our boats at the show, and took enough orders to make Fred rich and keep our factory humming for the next two years. After three downward inflection points, we had had our transformative moment.

There was a commercial on television in the early days of e-commerce that showed four young computer geeks going live with their website and cheering a moment later when the first order for their product came in. Ding! Exhilaration followed a string of orders. Ding, ding, ding! But as the orders came flooding in, dingdingding-dingdingdingdingdingdingdingdingdingdingdingdingding, their demeanor changed to concern and then fear and then panic as they realized they did not have the infrastructure to keep up with the unexpected demand. At Scout Boats, we never quite reached the point of panic, because we were dealing with retailers, not the general public, and dealers are realistic about the timelines of boatbuilding, but we did understand the imperative facing us of scaling up quickly while maintaining the quality and reliability that were and would be the hallmarks of our company.

The next couple of days were a whirlwind during which I spent all my time blowing up our business plan and developing a replacement for the next twenty-four months. Ecstatic, I informed Dianne at the dinner table that we would sell an astonishing $880,000 worth of boats that year, quadruple the previous projection. She thought that was preposterous and laughed so hard she nearly fell off her chair. As it turns out, I had missed the mark by a wide margin, as we billed another $300,000 more than that. In just our third year of existence, we earned $1.2 million in revenue and were primed to exceed that lofty figure the following year.

Having demand in the bank is bracing for a business because it provides ballast to the operation as it expands. We could plan our growth, which was going to be steep and immediate, and prepare for the significant changes that were about to take place in our company, and we could prepare for the next iteration of the journey, whatever that might prove to be. We earned a profit and beat those 197:3 odds despite vigorous protestations from Mother Nature and the initial opinion of the boating market. We became the elite 1.5 percent of successful start-ups, a steep climb from the abyss we had faced three times in our short tenure and as recently as a few months before the Atlanta show. Those were heady days, not quite yet a time to take stock, which we wouldn't have had time to do anyway, but three-

and-a-half decades later it is staggering to reminisce about the thin reed of timing and luck that separated us from complete, abject, and, likely permanent, failure. We were still up to bat despite three strikes, but even the most thick-headed umpire will send you to the dugout after four strikes.

A side note on the 172SF model that altered our trajectory and transformed the boating world: That model is still to this day our best-selling model, even though we phased it out in 2005 and replaced it with our popular 175SF. No one could have blamed us if we had named our firstborn child 172SF, but our kids had already been born.

The winding road that ultimately led to our success explains my discomfort with the term *Boat Boy*, which I've co-opted as the title of the book in order to take control of the phrase and redefine it. In one sense, I am the ultimate boat boy, having built, driven, and raced boats from my early childhood, even earning a living at it when I should have been attending school. Boatbuilding has literally been the only job I have ever had—the alpha and omega of my career and the source of every dollar I have ever earned. I have served literally every function in a boatbuilding operation, from janitor to CEO, and boats have broken my heart, swelled my pride, and filled my purse—but not before I put my family's finances and my reputation at the brink of destruction. My wife and children, and their spouses, have all joined me in the business, and today we oversee an innovative company, respected in the industry, that has earned nine patents, provided a living to 500 other families, brought joy to tens of thousands of boat owners, produced millions of dollars in economic activity, and over the years paid millions of dollars in taxes. We enjoy unusual engagement and loyalty among our team members, but even those staff who seek their fortune elsewhere have learned and grown in our shop and moved on to lucrative careers in a variety of industries, passing on the values we hold dear—quality, excellence, teamwork, perseverance, respect, and tolerance—to all those whom they encounter. Profitability is the trophy of success, but it isn't the most important by-product. Building something that will live beyond you is humbling and gratifying. The desire to see the business continue and prosper long after I'm gone has prompted me to work on a succession plan for the past two decades.

All that is true. At the same time, *Boat Boy* makes it all sound as if anyone with the background I just described would naturally build a $100 million company of highly respected boats known for their craftsmanship and dependability. As if I built a boat one day and a company sprang full grown from it, like Athena in Greek mythology emerging as an adult in full battle armor from Zeus's brow. It makes light of the trials and tribulations we endured, the full-throttle and relentless pursuit of quality, and the hard work of all the people, both before and after the establishment of the company, whose contributions made it the success it is today.

We had six dealers selling our boats going into the Atlanta show and thirty-seven exiting it, the difference between staying afloat and becoming a player in the industry. That changed my whole outlook at the time. Until that point, the purpose of the company was for Dianne and me to make a living doing what we loved. Despite all the evidence to the contrary, I never wavered in my belief that we could achieve that small measure of success. Atlanta shattered that belief and replaced it with the recognition that this enterprise had grown much bigger than just us. We were about to be responsible for many families' livelihoods. Into the bouillabaisse of emotions went the unexpected one of responsibility. I was soon going to feel responsible not just for my family's future, which was an awesome responsibility itself, but for many others' as well. When they take on employees, business owners assume an emotional burden that is difficult to convey on the job. Studies have revealed that managers tasked with layoffs suffer more emotionally than the individuals who are terminated. It's hard to believe until you're thrust into a position of authority and responsibility for a flock of people.

While we were broke heading into Atlanta, the months ahead allowed us to build liquidity along with boats. There is a funny irony to being in the boat business and not being liquid, but it is all too common. Our experience was not totally representative of the immense capital requirements of entering a business in which one item might cost six figures. Undercapitalization is one of the most common mistakes start-ups make, and it is fatal in a business whose financial barriers to entry are steep. Our new situation necessitated a move to larger headquarters and a rash of hirings, a standardized training system, and the development of a human resources infrastructure. Managing growth, particularly during the sort of rapid growth that became imperative at Scout in early 1991, is fraught with danger that can sink even a company faced with rising demand, so it was critical that we find individuals who shared our drive and passion to produce great boats like no other on the market, with brilliant new features, unquestioned dependability, and gorgeous styling. We took pains to surround ourselves with the right people, because it became evident that our main work was no longer boatbuilding; it was company building. Get that wrong and your boatbuilding company will find itself in another ironic situation: underwater.

I have learned many business lessons over the years, often catalogued as little bon mots or slogans that everyone at Scout Boats can repeat in their sleep, all of which I co-opted from others smarter than I. One of them is the KISS theory—keep it simple, stupid. Our boats have always been many great things—functional, reliable, beautifully handmade, innovative, sturdy, and good looking. We have created more "found features"—that is, new features previously unseen on boats that make the boating experience easier or more enjoyable—than any other company. One thing I have always insisted, though, is that they remain simple. We never want our machines to become so complicated that they can fail offshore and leave our customers stranded. In fact, my oldest son has worked his way up to vice president of product development, and he and his team repeatedly create brilliant new additions to our boats that are too sophisticated and complicated to be included. It's a great place to be, actually, because they remain unjaded and continuously push the envelope on boatmaking. This kind of unfettered creativity is critical to the long-lasting success of the enterprise. When a business loses its hunger, it begins to stagnate and die, like a shark that fails to move forward. Having been around as long as I have, you come to realize the balancing act necessary between the relentless quest to develop cutting-edge technology and the caution required not to create products that are so complex that your owners can no longer operate them.

Critical to this calculation is understanding in atomic detail who your customer is. The marketing world identifies brand personas: an individual representation of the characteristics that would describe a typical customer. No brand persona covers every customer, but if you focus on that target audience, everyone who shares the psychographic and behavioristic characteristics will likely follow. In other words, if you're marketing Bruce Springsteen concert tickets, you will focus on an audience that was attending high school during his glory days, because those are the people most likely to purchase tickets. A Boss fan in their thirties whose parents played his music while they were growing up will find the tickets despite not being part of the target market because they behave like the target audience in their radio and streaming-service listening habits. Because our boats cost $40,000 to $6 million, we start our brand persona with a higher-income individual, usually male, well-educated, and likely successful in business—someone who lives on the coast and is likely over forty. Our buyers value quality and view their boat as an investment; they are concerned with the level of depreciation this expensive asset will experience. They investigate all their options, do their homework on resale value, and are willing to pay more for high quality. They buy Scouts for practical reasons like dependability; for aesthetic reasons like the broken line of our hull that gives it a retro shape; and for lifestyle reasons like the ability to spend a chill day with the children or grandchildren on the water or share a few brews with the boys while fishing. Our customers value family time and want a boat that does the same.

CHAPTER 5

Build What's Never Been Built ... As Long As It's Scout-Worthy

The Atlanta show was the ultimate inflection point for our business, the moment that began an ever-upward arc to success at the personal level, then the family level, then the industry level, and now the legacy level. Though we have ridden the macroeconomic waves in thirty-plus years since, we have never experienced anything like the tripartite storms of Newport, Hugo, and the eleven-inch snowstorm that preceded Atlanta. There were three of us when it all came together in 1990 and still only seven by 1992 when we moved into much larger digs at a refurbished warehouse on the site of an abandoned airport. We were selling a couple of million dollars' worth of boats by then, and it had already become clear to me that the vision of a successful business that I could pass down to my kids and grandchildren had been realized. That is, I knew that Scout wasn't going away.

I was always a very analytical person. I guess what we call today a strategic thinker, but I always just considered that thinking. I don't really understand nonstrategic thinking. That's more like instinct, which doesn't particularly well prepare modern humans for the business world. There isn't much confluence between gathering berries or sticking a spear in a woolly mammoth and determining market shifts or anticipating consumer preferences. Besides that, I was taught by my various mentors to plan, plan, plan. After a long, glorious romance that served us both well over the years, I eventually became one with my spreadsheets and promiscuously flaunted that relationship in front of coworkers. Before the Atlanta show, I had spent voluminous hours every week building spreadsheets, estimating, revising, and developing plans. I was doing this one week at a time because we could hardly see beyond that, but in the immediate aftermath of the Atlanta show, the plan for my first week was to develop a plan for the next year.

That week-to-week stuff wasn't going to fly anymore. Our schedule, for as long as we could conceive, was about to switch from deliberate haste to turbocharged, foot pinned to the floor on the accelerator. Only, once I had sketched out the plans for the supplies of fiberglass, resin, wood, hardware, electrical components, and so on; estimated cash flow; determined labor usage and the need to upstaff; and calculated how my time and Dianne's would be best used, it became clear: If we were going to face the very bright but somewhat daunting future, we were going to have to spend more time running the business and less time conceptualizing new models and building them.

I spent the entire Christmas break on this project and was so proud of the monument to planning I had produced—really, an epic spreadsheet worthy of at least a nomination to the Excel Hall of Fame—that I was able to project our sales for the following year. I did a magnificent job of underestimating revenue by $320,000, or 36.4 percent, so detailed and exacting was my plan. Of course, this is a mostly wonderful problem to have, and I was grateful, despite the discrediting of my planning prowess that accompanied it.

While I was hard at work miscalculating our future and focusing on little more than building what had been ordered, Dianne was continuing her role of best partner any man could hope for. She had my back at every turn, supporting my vision, dream, desire, and goal to construct a boatbuilding company my way, answerable to nobody but the marketplace. I was determined to not do all the stupid things I had learned not to do, and Dianne was determined to help me get there. She spent those first weeks after Atlanta gluing, caulking, buffing—whatever needed to be done so that the actual boatbuilding never paused. We hired someone to help us with the detail work, and the owner of the barn in which we were operating built us a new, larger warehouse to accommodate our growth. Little did he know that our growth would very quickly expand by an order of several magnitudes.

At that point, I could not have envisioned what we now have, even though I was building it, with the help of many others, of course. Until recently, I've always pressed my nose hard to the grindstone and have been so focused on our daily challenges and short-term victories that I rarely looked beyond the next few months, let alone years. Perhaps this dedication to the daily grind and immediate tasks might explain our success: We've grown 12 percent annually, avoided debt, and increased boat production and staff, only faltering briefly during the Great Recession.

Even when the boat market suddenly dried up for a couple of years, we didn't just hunker down. Instead, we used that lull to innovate, crafting new models and features. While our competitors shed staff and waited out the storm, we kept busy. So when sales finally rebounded, we hit the water with fresh designs, outpacing the competition and emerging even stronger than before.

Widely considered to be one of the greatest professional football players of all time, Tom Brady has said that the journey is supposed to be hard because life is hard. To be successful one must be willing to endure the grind. "The truth is—you don't have to be special. You just have to be what most people aren't: consistent, determined, and willing to work for it. No shortcuts."[5]

I do feel like I was special in this sense: I am addicted to building boats. Even in my version of heaven on earth—sitting on a boat under a blue sky with a drink in one hand and a fishing rod in the other, family and beloved friends around me, and the song of the ocean as the soundtrack—the wheels in my head won't stop spinning.

When everyone else is enjoying the ultimate in relaxation, I'm quietly obsessing about how the boat's finish might be finer, the amenities might be upgraded, the ride made smoother or the electronics more convenient. Boatbuilding is such a part of me that it courses through my veins and monopolizes my idle thoughts, and when your synapses spend sixteen hours a day firing off thoughts about the process, it's going to lead to new ideas, improvements, and innovations. One need not be especially insightful: Even a blind squirrel finds an acorn now and then. If just one out of a hundred thoughts turns out to be productive, that is a lot of fodder for R&D. In a way, it's merely a numbers game; the greater the supply of seeds, the more wheat that will grow. Separating the wheat from the chaff is just process.

---

5 Leadership Now, "Tom Brady: To Be Successful at Anything, You Don't Have to Be Special," Leading Blog, June 22, 2024, https://www.leadershipnow.com/leadingblog/2024/06/tom_brady_to_be_successful_at.html.

Here's another similarity between an uber successful sports star and a humble entrepreneur made good—they both recognize the power of teamwork. "It wasn't me. It wasn't you. It was us," Brady told his coach, Bill Belichick, at his Patriots Hall of Fame induction. "Nothing in life of significance is ever accomplished alone."[6] There are probably many successful people out there who embrace the "self-made individual" trope, but it's more like tripe. No one in the history of the world ever made it alone. One can't build a company without ... a company. Without trusted managers and dedicated employees and fearless advisers. Without mentors and supporters and believers.

I've had my own driving forces: a wife who's been everything, kids who've pitched in, a mother's unwavering support, and a father whose approval came so late it only fueled my determination to prove him wrong. But let's not get too full of ourselves. Remember: Cemeteries are filled with indispensable people.

I don't know Tom Brady—Ed Marinaro is the closest I've gotten to friendship with football royalty—but I have no doubt that he would humbly acknowledge the similarities.

Scout Boats, which now employs five hundred people, including all three of our children, their spouses, a sister-in-law, a nephew, a fifteen-year-old grandson, and other family members, continues to exceed our wildest dreams.

We never aimed to be the biggest or sell the most boats. That ambition might've ruined us, forcing us to abandon our core values. Instead, Dianne and I simply wanted to create a business that could support our family and showcase what a truly great boat could

---

6 Michael David Smith, "Tom Brady Tells Bill Belichick: 'It Wasn't Me, It Wasn't You, It Was Us,'" NBC Sports, June 13, 2024, https://www.nbcsports.com/nfl/profootballtalk/rumor-mill/news/tom-brady-tells-bill-belichick-it-wasnt-me-it-wasnt-you-it-was-us

be: beautifully designed, long lasting, and reasonably priced. We wanted to prove it could be built, marketed, and sold without compromise. We know "reasonable" is relative. Our least expensive boat still requires a hefty investment, plus ongoing costs. It's a far cry from the $800 aluminum fishing boats or the nearly free used ones you might find. Those serve a purpose, but they're a different world from what we build. We've often wished our boats could be within reach for the average family, but that's not the market we ended up serving. Our niche is for those who want to venture further, safely.

For our company, while the logarithmic growth has not been intentional, the underlying principles have never been in doubt. I believed from the start, and now know to be true for sure, that sticking to values and vision above all offers the best odds for business success. Nothing leads to failure like veering from principles, no matter how expedient or lucrative that seems in the short run.

If you ask Scout owners what attributes led them to purchase our product in a crowded marketplace of competitors, their answers will tend to congregate around a handful of concepts. Reliability, dependability, stylish design, and value retention are the common impressions. But the granddaddy of them all is innovation, because it is the engine that drives all the others.

Continuous improvement has been our mantra from day one, the wellspring of all our success. It's as if W. Edwards Deming's ghost walks our factory floor with us. Deming, the father of total quality management, revolutionized industry worldwide, particularly in postwar Japan. He died at ninety-three just as we were starting up, but by then his ideas had become gospel in the business world. The sharklike "move forward or die" mentality he inspired has ruled for half a century now. Though I never read Deming directly, his principles were drilled into me early on and became part of Scout Boats' foundational elements from day one.

I've never done a psychological workup on myself, but writing a book tends to force one to turn inward for insights. It's obvious that the early years spent dedicating myself to the craft of boatbuilding—when I wasn't perfecting my pickup lines on short women—helped lead to the unimaginable success we have experienced. Choosing the management track with Dave Stanton in the '70s, despite the initial pay cut, was pivotal. It armed me with skills crucial for founding and growing a company, especially one so dedicated to its foundational principles. That job, focused on teaching people to build seaworthy, low-maintenance boats, ingrained in me the importance of quality—now a Scout Boats hallmark.

There is no question that experiencing the support and mentorship of so many people in my career prepared me to value great employees, to offer them continuing education and mentorship, and to promote from within almost exclusively. Experiencing poor management, absent leadership, short-sighted corporate greed, mistreatment of staff, disengaged employees, a lack of commitment to quality, and almost every other pathology of American business life imbued me with a fanatical psychological obsession to create and execute the opposite.

Every month, we gather the staff for a half hour of recognition and inspiration, during which a couple of minutes are reserved for me to say a few words. I often remind them that nothing short of 100 percent quality is acceptable, that our customers deserve nothing less than our fanatical obsession with building boats that take their breath away and increase their enjoyment on the water. I remind them that by adhering to these demands they create for themselves a status unavailable to them in any other endeavor.

Consider this. Among our five hundred employees, we do not have a single Olympic gold medalist in anything, not even curling. Not one of us is a number one bestseller of even a cookbook (that I am aware of), has written a number one song on the Billboard chart, has won a world championship in any competitive undertaking, or has been crowned Mr. or Miss Universe. Despite my own basketball christening at the local Jewish community center in which my mother enrolled me as a youth, I am, at five foot six, utterly devoid of ability at hoops. (Being bad at basketball and not Jewish would seem to be a double whammy, but the folks at the community center didn't seem put off by either. Another nice life lesson.)

Working together, though, we have an opportunity every day to build the world's greatest boats. By fixating on quality of construction and fit and finish, by adding the most innovative elements and amenities, by standing behind everything we build, every one of our five hundred team members can proudly assert that they are the best boatbuilder in the world. I remind my employees all the time that we have many customers who are gazillionaires and can buy any kind of boat they want, and they choose Scouts. We sold six highly customized boats to the royal family of Qatar, from the richest family on the planet. He lives halfway around the world, but he chose us. It's something to be proud of and to live up to every day. I know that most of our employees wear Scout on their sleeve, buy into this commitment, and are driven by the success of the business. To intensify that connection, we offer a very generous profit-sharing plan. The success of our business over the past thirty years has poured significant income into the pockets of our loyal team members, and that deeply gratifies me.

This total team commitment reminds me of a famous interaction between the president of the United States in the 1960s and a janitor at the new NASA headquarters in Houston. Following the Soviet Union's successful manned space flight, President John Kennedy had committed the nation to putting a man on the moon by the end of the decade. Moving this dream to fruition required a massive budgetary commitment and a herculean effort by some of the nation's top aerospace engineers. (Unlike most life endeavors, this was in fact rocket science.) When NASA's managers brought the president in for a peek at their progress, a PR ploy designed to keep the largess flowing from Washington, they were mortified to see the building's janitor rush up and intercept Kennedy. The charming commander-in-chief shook the hand of his admirer and mortified the managers further by asking him about his role at NASA. Nearly apoplectic, they could just imagine this low-paid employee describing for the leader of the free world his role in cleaning the toilets. Instead, the janitor replied, "Mr. President, I'm helping to put a man on the moon." There was likely not much that an uneducated Black man in segregated 1962 Texas could boast about, but he could take pride in his role in the only successful program to land human beings on another celestial body. Although our team members thankfully have many more opportunities in life than the janitor had, and our efforts are far humbler than landing people on the moon, they take similar pride in being great at what we do.

One way we accomplished that in the early years was to hire great people. Not great boatbuilders or great—whatever the job was—but great people. We brought on many unskilled individuals who were unpretentious and possessed what these days is called a growth mindset. They wanted to learn and didn't let their ego get in the way. Many of them didn't even have résumés. In fact, they hardly had anything including job opportunities, but they had character, the kind of thing we needed to build a cohesive team. The good people we hired brought their siblings and cousins and friends, and I could tell in a job interview how much the people I was interviewing moved the needle on motivation and ego. I wanted to pin the meter on the former and barely see the needle move on the latter. It's hard to fake that stuff in an interview, and with my BS detector on red alert, I was able to determine who would fit in and who wouldn't pretty quickly. Today, of course, we have a whole department that handles this work, with keywords and AI scrubbing of job applications and all the modern technology in hiring, but we haven't budged from our work to bring in quality individuals who want to sacrifice for a team and do fulfilling work.

That is the justification for promoting from within as much as possible. Over the years we have opened whole new departments whose staff mix required outside expertise, but for the most part, we want to know that our team leaders, supervisors, managers, directors, vice presidents, and other leaders in the organization are great fits for the company who demonstrate what these days we would call high social-emotional IQ. As a growing enterprise, there are tremendous opportunities at Scout Boat, and I strongly encourage promoting from within. It's come back to bite us a couple of times, but we have learned our lessons and developed a method that works quite well. We've had people who lit the world on fire as, say, a team leader, whom we grabbed by the shoulders and said, "You're such a superstar doing this; we're going to make you a supervisor," and then they fell flat on their faces. When the Peter principle takes hold, it's a pickle for the company and the employee, because there's no such thing as going back. That would be demoralizing and humiliating for the employee and send a terrible message to the crew—that if you work hard and move up and fail, you're busted to a lower position, or out the door.

After a couple of those lose-lose situations that created stress and pain for everyone, which I should mention were vastly outweighed by all the great promotions from within that have worked well, we learned a new strategy. We still promote from within obsessively, but we hedge our bets to give the employee time to acclimate and give us time to evaluate. We'll tell the employee that we need someone to fill in temporarily and want them to do so on a trial basis. Then, on the rare occasions that it reveals a side of the person we hadn't previously recognized, we can slide them back to their old positions as if it were the most natural thing in the world. As I've said repeatedly, I've been successful in business mostly because I've learned what not to do.

Folks often ask how those lean early years shaped our success. They wonder: Did Dianne and I thrive because of those setbacks, or in spite of them? Did they mold us in any discernible way, harden our outer shell, steel us against future misfortune, instill in us added motivation to show the world it couldn't stop us? Not being a psychologist or even engaging in much of this kind of self-examination, I think all that has cause and effect reversed. Dianne and I were just totally dedicated to building a business, we knew we could do it, and we already possessed relentless natures that wouldn't allow us to give up. You can decide for yourself where you stand on the nature-nurture debate, but we were both lucky enough to carry a psychological toolbox that included persistence.

I didn't know—I still don't know—anything but boatbuilding; I knew I was good at it and that I never wanted to return to working for someone else. That didn't leave us much alternative but to fight through the obstacles until the stars better aligned for us. We put everything on the line in Atlanta and were ecstatic about how that show worked out, but the truth is that we knew we had something special to offer the industry even before we embarked and were confident going in that there would be demand for our products. It was not a surprise at all that the show catapulted us to profitability; only the scope of the success surprised us. Had we enjoyed much more modest success, had we emerged with just six more dealers—i.e., doubled our representation—our company would have almost inevitably grown and succeeded from there because we built great boats that people wanted. Signing on thirty-one dealers from that show simply shifted the paradigm all at once and all but guaranteed far faster growth and profit, which itself can be a double-edged sword if the business does not adapt. The dramatic results of Atlanta changed the scale of our operation but not our trajectory. We already were convinced that was pointed upward.

Part of the company ethos that has ensured continued growth has been the relentless pursuit of creativity rather than mimicry. We are always experimenting, tinkering, seeking something new and better, and trendsetting features to improve form and function, so when rivals finally adopt our most recent innovation, we have moved on to the next one. That has been as true with our modest 14-foot fishing boats as with our multimillion-dollar 67-foot yachts. (Okay, maybe not quite as true, but the ethos is the same.) Our list of innovations could fill a chapter and cure your insomnia for all time, but it takes up residence in a research and development team that is part of our company, not outsourced to some other company, as some in the boatbuilding industry prefer. Our hulls are designed in house, not outsourced, allowing us to create a unique modern aesthetic while maintaining their primary function.

Our adventurous R&D team has invented much of today's state of the art in boatbuilding. Our Scout stepped hull technology enables boats to move smoothly through the water for superior passenger comfort and fuel efficiency. Our epoxy infusion construction involves impregnating fiberglass and other composite materials with a resin mixture, resulting in a lighter, stronger, and more durable final product compared to traditional boat construction methods. One of my favorite innovations was our patent-earning articulating "rocket launcher" fishing rod storage unit. When the R&D team generally, and my son specifically, mentioned this innovation to me, I scoffed. It was way too complicated and added too little utility, contributed electronics that the boat owner wouldn't be able to fix, and just seemed unnecessary and cumbersome. But Stevie persisted, and now I can't imagine our boats without them.

Here's how the rocket launcher works. Every boat has slender tubes that hold fishing rods on the boat. When we developed electrically controlled blinds that owners could deploy to enclose the deck, the fishing rods were in the way. Our R&D team solved that problem by developing a system to digitally articulate the tubes 90 degrees so the rods are horizontal and the blinds can come out. One button controls all of it. Despite my initial misgivings, the team's innovation earned "wows" on all three elements—idea, function, and aesthetic—and has become a staple of our boats, earning kudos throughout the boating industry.

We get a lot of that, actually. The boating press loves our creations and are always eager to hear about the latest innovation we have added, much the way the tech press awaits each new iPhone and fawns over its groundbreaking features. As with the automobile industry, the constant pressure to improve and innovate drives us every day, so that a 2025 model will be nothing like a 1995 model.

Consider a new car today, which comes standard with satellite radio, a backup camera to help bad drivers steer in reverse, a smart key that can find your vehicle in a crowded parking lot, lane protection to keep the car from sliding into the adjacent lane, plug-in and hybrid batteries to boost gas mileage or eliminate the need for gas altogether, Bluetooth integration so we don't operate our phones while driving, radar-based cruise control, GPS navigation, 360-degree airbags, stability control, and so much more that was not available in 1995. It is the same in the boat business, and as the leader in developing new features, we don't subscribe to the axiom that "if it ain't broke, don't fix it." We break every model and attempt to put it back together even better so that our customers can always be confident that the current model is the most advanced, convenient, efficient version we have ever offered. Our models get updated before we've sold one thousand of them. In contrast, Ford will deliver 750,000 F-series trucks this year in the US alone.

This is a big part of the reason that our boats must be made by hand: It's not possible to amortize the cost to purchase and program a robot over just six thousand boats. The result is that all our boats are built by hand in Summerville, South Carolina, by Americans of every race, creed, color, sex, gender, sexual orientation, political affiliation, family situation, and background. I'll talk more about how we build our team a little later, but the one takeaway here is that our boats are built with human hands and brains, fat tubes of elbow grease, and a whole lot of heart.

Every one of our Scout models features 100 percent hand-laid fiberglass construction or infusion, finished bilges, lids, hatches, and door undersides. We pioneered the first reverse-shoebox hull/deck design, increasing overall hull strength and preventing water from penetrating the hull/deck joint in rough conditions. We build gas-saving hulls with a whole host of state-of-the-art outboard engine advancements, including mounting systems that offer the best strength-to-weight ratio of any boat in its class. We have pushed the industry above 60 percent fuel efficiency, and when our competitors finally reach that threshold, we will be pushing the standard even higher. We were the first to install fully digital dashboards despite the dire warnings of everyone in the industry, and we offer heated seats, hardtop-mounted solar panels, anchor, cameras and much more. A couple of these innovations have made their way on to our boats over my objections.

Okay, that was a sop to the marketing team—two paragraphs of bragging and now I'm done, except to say that was a partial list, and I apologize to all those who revolutionized some other area of boatmaking or another that I have failed to include, not because it isn't a magnificent step forward but because I don't want to lose the reader, who expected this book to be presented without commercial interruption. Let's just say I'm very proud of the boats we build—you'll never hear me call them units—and the joy we can provide our customers, as well as the safety and comfort we surround them in when they embark on the water for the sublime experience that is one of the two things that have given my life meaning. Family is the other, of course. I'm even prouder of the company we built to produce those great boats, a company of people—five hundred people as I write this—who put their hearts and souls into their work, meaningful work that enables them to create their own families, live well, and thrive.

I believe, but don't know for sure, that we have earned the most patents in the industry, and if somehow that isn't true, we certainly have earned the most per employee or revenue or whatever other metric for size you want to apply—and by a wide margin.

All of which brings us to one of my favorite subjects: nepotism! Establishing a business that your children and their families can join if they so desire is an indescribable blessing, but giving them anything they haven't earned is a curse, not just on them but on the business and your other team members. We have walked that tightrope and found our way to the other side, without any fatal false steps, at least so far, but it has required forethought, planning, and hard decisions.

CHAPTER 6

The Kids Join the Team

The story behind the Scout name might raise some eyebrows. It harks back to my early days at the Outboard Shop, where I first learned to build boats called Scouts. This was around the time I started shaving, and I earned a princely sum of four bucks an hour. In 1967, that wage was something to brag about. Minimum wage hovered around a buck twenty, and the median weekly household income sat at $138. As a tenth grader—when I bothered to show up for class—I could match a full-time working dad's weekly pay in just seventeen hours. It felt like striking gold.

The short answer is that the Scout name was available, and I liked it. The longer story is that those little Scouts ignited my career as well as my boat addiction, and they afforded a fifteen-year-old who had basically stopped going to school the opportunity to outearn grown men while learning a profitable trade. Those Scouts were held in high esteem in the business because many owners of high-end Bertrams and Boston Whalers also owned Scouts and used them as tenders to transport themselves back and forth from their luxury cruisers. The name Scout was a thread in the tangled web of my youthful adventure, tinged with romance and greed, status, and power that marked my life at a fraught time in any boy's development when everything seems bigger and more important. I was a little baby-faced kid with a part-time father, a distaste for formal education, and a penchant for the waves that called out to me every day on the South Carolina coast, and those Scouts were my nectar.

The Outboard Shop quit making Scouts in the early 1970s and sold out to the owner of the now-defunct Piggly Wiggly Carolina Company in 1971. Why a grocery chain wanted to own a boatbuilding company, I don't recall, but company president Buzzy Newton knew enough to steer clear of the boatbuilding industry, and the Outboard Shop dissolved along with the Scout name. Two decades later when I returned from Newport with my tail between my legs and a pile of unsold tenders on my trailer, I reminisced about those Scouts that I loved so well and decided to build them and rechristen the company with the name that sparked such nostalgia in me. Sometime after that, Newton sniffed around about my right to use the name, prompting me to trademark the brand. Some years later the Boy Scouts raised a ruckus, and after protracted negotiations and our bilateral initiative to keep a gaggle of lawyers in Rolex watches, we agreed that I could maintain my company name as long as I didn't teach young males to build fires without matches or navigate by the stars ... or some such thing. Our businesses don't overlap at all, and one would think a five-minute conversation and a handshake could have settled the name issue, but that's how business gets done in America in the twenty-first century and the reason I receive lovely Christmas cards from several attorneys annually.

All that was long before my children were old enough to think about careers; indeed, my youngest daughter was a toddler at this point. Having returned from Atlanta in triumph, Dianne and I knew the business would survive and even thrive, but we didn't yet know for sure the shape and scope of that success. Nonetheless, it was always our intention to build something that we could pass down to our kids, and thus the very moment we could wrangle my son into the business we did, starting him at the very bottom, just as I had, and allowing him to learn the business tactically at first, then strategically while he attended high school. Though my own charmed life involved an exchange of formal education for on-the-job learning, Dianne and I were adamant that our children dedicate themselves to their studies and afford themselves the full array of opportunities, whether that included boatbuilding or not.

Our middle daughter, Sherrie, graduated from Clemson and ran an upscale café called Potts of Coffee until she got married and decided the sixty-hour work weeks were not conducive to raising a family. She has labored her way up to lead our HR department, a part of the business that I know precious little about and for which I am eternally grateful that we employ a department of people with expertise I don't have. Our youngest, Stephanie, attended the College of Charleston and earned a master's in teaching art at the University of South Carolina (thanks, kids, for those in-state tuition bills!) and taught in a local school district for a while before joining us a decade ago and working her way up in the accounting department to serve as controller.

And as I've mentioned, our oldest, Stevie, came aboard at age fourteen, much as I had, working in the laminating department for three dollars an hour. Like me, an introvert whose hands do his talking, he opted to spend his summers working alongside everyone else, learning all the aspects of the business and earning the stray shekel. His creative juices were most stoked by imagining new ways to make boat owning an ever more transcendent joy, and so he joined the R&D department, which he could see was the driving force in the company. After two decades at Scout Boats, he's now running that shop, probably the worst position in the company, because it's the one job in the business that the pain-in-the-neck founder still thinks he can do and is willing to meddle in. I can't tell my daughters how to handle accounting or employee benefits, but my poor son and his compatriots must do the hard work of creation with the old man looking over their shoulders—or under their armpits, since I'm still the guy towered over by five-foot-four women in heels.

In each case, my children entered the business the same way all the other first hires did—at the level of their skills and experience. Although we have carved out positions in management for family members, none of them attained those roles without apprenticing at lower levels along the way. Both my son and my grandson, now fifteen, started at the very bottom, gluing fiberglass over molds. Stevie, my son, worked a series of jobs in the business until he discovered his passion for the creative side, moved into the R&D department, and honed his skills over twenty years before ascending to a leadership role there. That feels natural, given that it's exactly the path my career followed, starting at the bottom in high school, learning every job in the factory, and then getting into management and working my way up there. I can say not just to my children and grandchildren but to everyone in the organization, "I understand what you're going through because I was in your position once upon a time."

Part of the company ethos is to treat everyone the same irrespective of all the irrelevant nonsense like their demographic background. Performance is all that matters in our shop, and those who buy into the values of the company—chief among them hard work, mutual respect, excellence, teamwork, persistence, and innovation—rise inside the company and share the fruits of our success. But I would be lying if I didn't acknowledge that this company was built for my family and they will own it when Dianne and I are gone. In fact, we have already transferred over almost half of the ownership to my three children, and the rest is coming in due time as part of our succession plan. It makes sense for them to occupy leadership positions in the company they own; how ludicrous would it be for one of my kids to be a one-third owner at age forty-five while sanding fiberglass on the shop floor or serving as a junior assistant in the marketing department?

I mentioned that my children have followed some of my footsteps aside from those that walked out the high school doors without a diploma. Both my parents were mortified that I quit school, but my father remained so even as my career took off. For most of his life, he thought I was a numbskull for neglecting my studies and remained confident that it would all come crashing down once my lack of academic credentials was discovered. Ironically, since he was a navy man, he didn't seem to understand that I was, in fact, quite focused on my studies—not of trigonometry, the Boer War, and French grammar, but of the sea, of watercraft, of fiberglass, resin, and epoxy, and most importantly, of business. It's a further irony that Dianne and I insisted that our children fully engage themselves in academics so that they would have options in life. We were supportive of their choices, though, and while my daughters both graduated from college and pursued their own careers, my son opted to step directly into the business following high school and has demonstrated a talent for its creative side.

My father did eventually come around begrudgingly when he witnessed what a success my business had become, and I am gratified to report that we enjoyed a renewed relationship in his later years once he fully recognized that I didn't turn out so terribly after all. My son brought into the family a fabulous daughter-in-law to whom he has remained married for eighteen years and gave my father two wonderful grandchildren of whom he was always proud. The journey wasn't always smooth sailing with my dad, but we reached our destination with our sails intact. I am grateful to have been his son; he introduced me to the water, and I haven't left it. My father, in fact, was my first mentor.

At the same time, there is no doubt my lack of academic credentials has exacted a personal toll on me. Though I was a whiz at math, I never did well at school because my heart wasn't in it. A big part of it was immaturity. For example, I couldn't understand the fascination with world history when I was fifteen, whereas I'm quite fascinated by it as an adult—but the other significant variable was just that I was so interested in boats. Dropping out worked for me then, but it has always felt like a stigma. As I became successful, I harbored a sense of inferiority toward highly educated people, in whose company I often travel when outside the factory. I have served on several multinational boards of directors like Wachovia and Wells Fargo, where I'm surrounded by Ivy Leaguers and other uber-educated people. It's intimidating, but also thrilling, because although I dropped out as a teenager, I have been a voracious student since.

I've never had an issue with lacking humility, particularly the humility to understand that I might learn something from another person, so I am eager to listen and learn from the scholars around the boardroom table. I've realized over time that I'm just as smart as any of them, though perhaps not as academically gifted, but whereas my expertise is boat manufacturing and the small number of adjacent disciplines, theirs are other areas of knowledge about which I likely know nothing, or close to it. So, I enjoy pushing their buttons and getting them to enlighten me in whatever is their area of luminescence. In many cases, my critical expertise, the one that provides me with a material advantage that boatbuilding does not, is the introvert's trick—the ability to coax conversation out of others in a manner that leads them to believe we have had a conversation, when in fact they did all the sharing. That is not something anyone teaches you at Harvard; you learn it in the school of life, from which I feel like I have graduated with a PhD.

Moving from our little barn to the upgraded twelve-thousand-square-foot building didn't alter our self-impression as upstarts in the recreational boating industry. After two years of steady growth that had us bursting at the seams in the upsized barn at the erstwhile airport, it was time to find larger accommodations. We purchased sixteen acres of nearby land from Clemson University and built our fifty-four-thousand-square-foot Plant A. When we moved two years later, we had grown fivefold. That day in late '96, when we first stepped into our gleaming new facility, hit me like a ton of bricks. We weren't just small-time anymore. We'd crossed some invisible line, diving headfirst into a whole new league of business.

Coming out of the Atlanta show, I was confident that the business would be viable. Sometime between then and Plant A I knew we would succeed as a competitive player in the luxury coastal fishing boat industry. The day we moved into Plant A cemented my growing feeling that we had built a successful brand and would be in business to stay. These were not epiphanies that occurred at a single moment like the apple hitting Isaac Newton on the head, and so they didn't feel like much of a revelation as they happened. Only in retrospect are we awed by the blizzard of good fortune, good decisions, and hard work that was required to climb that mountain and plant that flag of legitimacy. I'm amazed looking back at how delirious we were to have come so far at that moment, and yet how very far we still had to go. With fifty-one employees we were a niche player one-tenth the size we are today. I was still a young man with teenage kids working twenty-five hours a day, eight days a week before I was able to step back for a moment and realize I had achieved my dream.

And then it was back to work.

In 1996 we debuted out 172 Dorado dual console. We outfitted it with some unusual elements for the time—an angled windshield and high-end stylings with fancy-colored foam-filled cushions only found in expensive luxury boats. Industry people once again thought we had dropped our marbles in the ocean and lost them for good, but those 17-footers were so popular that Boston Whaler mimicked our design the following year and won Boat of the Year. We recognized that buyers wanted versatile products for family recreation, not salty fishing boats for good old boys to bang around in. We built boats to take fishing or to a restaurant on the harbor. We knew that there was a renaissance coming in our industry and by positioning ourselves on the leading edge we could stay one model year ahead of everyone else, boosting both our reputation and our sales. That 17-footer to this day is the best-selling boat we've ever manufactured.

Opening Plant A and unveiling the 172 Dorado conveyed to us another seminal moment in our evolution—our first news conference. We onboarded a PR firm that recommended we gather the industry media upon the release of the 172 Dorado and show off our startling new creation. As I've mentioned, I was not built for grand pronouncements before mass gatherings with our reputation on the line. I am much more comfortable with a roll of fiberglass and some resin, or on the water with my leading lady and the family she has bequeathed me. But when you have something to say and you know why it is important, it's easier to stand before the snarling media and answer questions. That first news conference had my nerves jangling from dinner the previous night right through the moment I walked on the stage, a feeling with which any introvert can identify. But with the boat standing proudly next to me, I knew she and I would survive because whatever I did or said, she was a beauty, and I could simply let her carry the conversation.

And that's exactly how it went.

I extolled the boat's virtues, and very quickly the tone of the furious throng from national boating magazines softened to curiosity. And then they nodded with interest. And then smiled with appreciation. The questions got friendlier, and I got the sense that we had won over the boating media, even as they pressed me with questions about daring to break conventions. Not only were the reviews stellar for that particular model, but the whole experience stoked the interest of the boating press thereafter for the latest innovations we would unveil.

Over the past twenty years we have garnered as much media attention for our boats as does Brunswick Boat Group, the world's largest builder of pleasure boats, dwarfing us with eighteen brands and annual sales of $2 billion and, not exactly coincidently, the owner of the iconic Boston Whaler brand. We'll get to what that is all about in a second, because I want to remain focused on how the boating media spend as much time writing about Scout Boats as Mercury, Sea Ray, Bayliner, Quicksilver, and all fourteen others combined, despite the mighty marketing muscle possessed by this one division of a $6 billion conglomerate. No one who has seen me deliver my lines would agree that I am being falsely modest when I argue that media representatives are not coming to hear me speak. This is not the Oracle of Omaha we're talking about—more like the Stutterer of Summerville. The Scout Boats secret is this: Every time we introduce a new boat, we introduce a new idea with it, and the boating industry press knows it will always walk away from one of our news conferences with something to write about. They can be confident that Scout is about to reveal some revolutionary design change, absolving the messenger of much of the responsibility of delivering an entertaining dog and pony show. We go with a "Just the facts, ma'am" approach that allows the latest innovations to speak for themselves. It's all part of our ethos of excellence.

It would be logical for my son to commandeer news conference duties from me, both because he and his team are the people responsible for the brilliant new designs I get to show off but also because it would demonstrate to the boating media and the marketplace at large that the company is maintaining or even accelerating its focus on innovation as it passes on to the next generation. I would be perfectly happy to hand over the reins, even though I have become comfortable handling front man duties. It is easy to be the designated storyteller when there is a good story to tell. But Stevie's story is one of a backbencher, a man behind the scenes who is indispensable but also invisible to the outside world. He's a great guy one on one, but standing in the limelight and speaking in public is not for him, and we all respect that. Eventually, as I reduce my involvement during my golden years, someone else is going to have to assume the mantle, but that is an issue for another day.

While I've already shared some information about our company and boats in the previous chapter, I could mention that we've received positive feedback from industry reviews. However, I'll refrain from quoting them here to avoid repetition. Suffice to say that we have earned a reputation for innovation, reliability, durability, sleekness, and performance in the marketplace that is probably my single greatest achievement after my family. It is one thing to believe in the product you produce but quite another for disinterested third parties to commend your work repeatedly and believe so strongly in your creativity that they await your next move with bated breath. Of course, none of that would mean anything if consumers didn't follow suit, but it turns out that the most discerning boat buyers are our best customers.

We have achieved all this in an unusual way. For better or worse, and I would contend it's mostly for worse, the vector of American business is toward consolidation. We see it in nearly every industry, from beverages to funeral homes, airlines to veterinary clinics, and eyeglasses to software, online search, and social media. Although there might be many brands in any given industry, they have all been gobbled up by a handful of companies wielding economies of scale and marketplace dominance, setting prices, and turning all of life into a soulless corporate endeavor. Sadly, this familiar story applies to the boatbuilding business, where a handful of companies have bought out the iconic brands like Bertram and Boston Whaler, and just about everyone else.

As in many industries, large players eventually run aground on innovation and deplete their organic growth capabilities. In order to quench their shareholders' voracious appetite for growth or to derail promising competitors who have introduced new and better ideas, they pressure smaller companies into merging (i.e., getting taken over) and in the process become larger inorganically. Often, the acquired company has little choice because it is getting squeezed by regulation and/or the market dominance of the larger players, and so it cashes in while it still can. This is common among physicians, for example, whose small practices are buckling under the weight of administrative costs stemming from insurance claims and healthcare rules. Almost any practice you visit today is owned by the local hospital, with its appointment-making and payment services centralized, often for greater convenience unless there is a problem. Then it's just another big bureaucracy where accessing a human is time consuming, difficult, and even futile.

Sometimes these buyouts involve synergies, as duplicate operations can be streamlined. Sometimes they can lower costs and reduce prices or improve service for consumers. But as the acquiring goliaths begin dominating the industry, they can take on monopolistic practices that limit choice and harm consumers. As I write this, a federal judge has just ruled that Google has acted as a monopolist by manipulating the marketplace so that it controls 97 percent of online searches in the US, and Apple, Amazon, Meta, Instagram, and WhatsApp all face antitrust litigation.

They came for Scout Boats, too, a tiny dot on the boating landscape, and I have entertained an offer or two just to understand our company's value and determine whether a merger might ever be in the best interest of our family and our employees. Having surveyed the landscape, I can say unequivocally that under current marketplace conditions, there is no scenario in which selling out to the corporate behemoth would benefit anyone connected to Scout Boats—including our customers. Corporations worry about satisfying shareholders first and foremost, obsess about quarterly profits, and generally treat employees as costs rather than assets. Although some understand that customers follow quality, they are more inclined to solve reduced sales with more aggressive marketing rather than reflecting on the quality of their products and considering the impacts of their decisions on a longer time horizon. Selling would probably lead to layoffs of whole departments whose work could be outsourced to corporate headquarters, disengagement from our company values, and the recasting of the business from a family legacy to an asset hardly different from gold bars or land, to be amortized, depreciated, bought, sold, and liquidated without concern for its provenance or legacy.

Bleh.

One reason we can skirt the private equity onslaught is because we bootstrapped the operation at the outset and have grown wisely and iteratively without debt. Our profits have always gone back into the company to facilitate the next phase of growth. Unlike other independent boat companies, we aren't operating under a crushing debt load that keeps the C-suite awake at night. With peace of mind, I'm not in a position where my cardiologist is encouraging me to sell before the pressure turns off the ticker. So, if you hear that Scout Boats is negotiating a buyout, that will be an indication that the marketplace has entered a new, regrettable phase in which it is impossible even for a small, nimble, debt-free, frame-breaking company with a positive internal culture to compete. Buy your boat before the deal is consummated because the balance of power will move from the customer to the shareholder once the takeover occurs.

I don't mean to suggest that is our future; I don't believe it is. Dianne and I have spent a lot of time succession planning, not just to navigate the business's passage from us to our children but also from them to their children. It's a widely used aphorism that the first generation builds the business, the second generation grows the business, and the third generation sinks the business. This is reminiscent of the small business seminar I attended where we were warned that only a couple of the people in a room of two hundred would build anything sustainable. That motivated me to persevere and beat the odds, and we're doing everything possible today to ensure the same for our business in the future. Five hundred families, the vast majority of them unrelated to us, depend on this operation for their livelihood and I'm going to do everything I can to ensure that their children and grandchildren continue to have that opportunity.

For fifteen years we have been succession planning, and each year there is more and more to disperse. We meet with our advisory committee semiannually, and each time we do, Dianne and I get killed off so we can determine what will happen next. (I hope to repeat this role-playing for another fifteen years.) We established an irrevocable trust to deflect the byzantine tax laws, and we sketch out the rough path forward for those upon whom the burden of directing Scout Boats will fall in our absence. We have deliberately crafted a plan for business continuation and not for a financial asset whose value can simply be spun off. Five hundred employees, tens of thousands of boating enthusiasts, and one legacy are all counting on Scout Boats remaining an innovative leader in the luxury coastal fishing boat market out to the twenty-second century.

Developing a succession plan requires a steely-eyed vision for the business, just as running the business has. There is no margin for misplaced sentimentality if you want your business to survive and thrive. If my kids or their spouses or others in our family were incompetent, I could not possibly allow them to rise to management positions. If I had somehow made that mistake, I would be forced to move them out or separate them from the company. The continued survival and growth of the company, along with its service to customers and its function as a source of livelihood for employees and long-term source of income and legacy for my family, are way more important than assuaging the ego of someone who either lacks the talent or motivation to succeed at a high level. That is why I have required all family members to prove their value in the company, starting at the level at which they are qualified and no higher, and earning their way to any management position. For my son, that meant literally gluing together fiberglass during summers as a teenager, and it's the same for my grandson today.

Much to the chagrin of family, particularly my wife, I have taken the same approach with the succession plan. None of my family serve as president of our company today, and I'm not sure what the future holds. That is not a comment on their abilities, but running a multimillion-dollar business is hard work with long hours that may not appeal to my son and daughters. They have good lives full of children and travel—and balance. This is a superb development in their lives, and it makes me very happy, frankly, that they do not share my debilitating addiction to boatbuilding. This disease has served our family very well in so many ways, but one addiction has been sufficient for about three generations of Pottses. Moreover, my children will be supremely well taken care of as owners of Scout Boats without having to labor day, night, and weekends on the moment-to-moment operational headaches of the business. This decision may cause a small amount of family strife, but I am secure enough to know that it is the best one for everyone, will serve my kids and future generations well, and will eventually win favor.

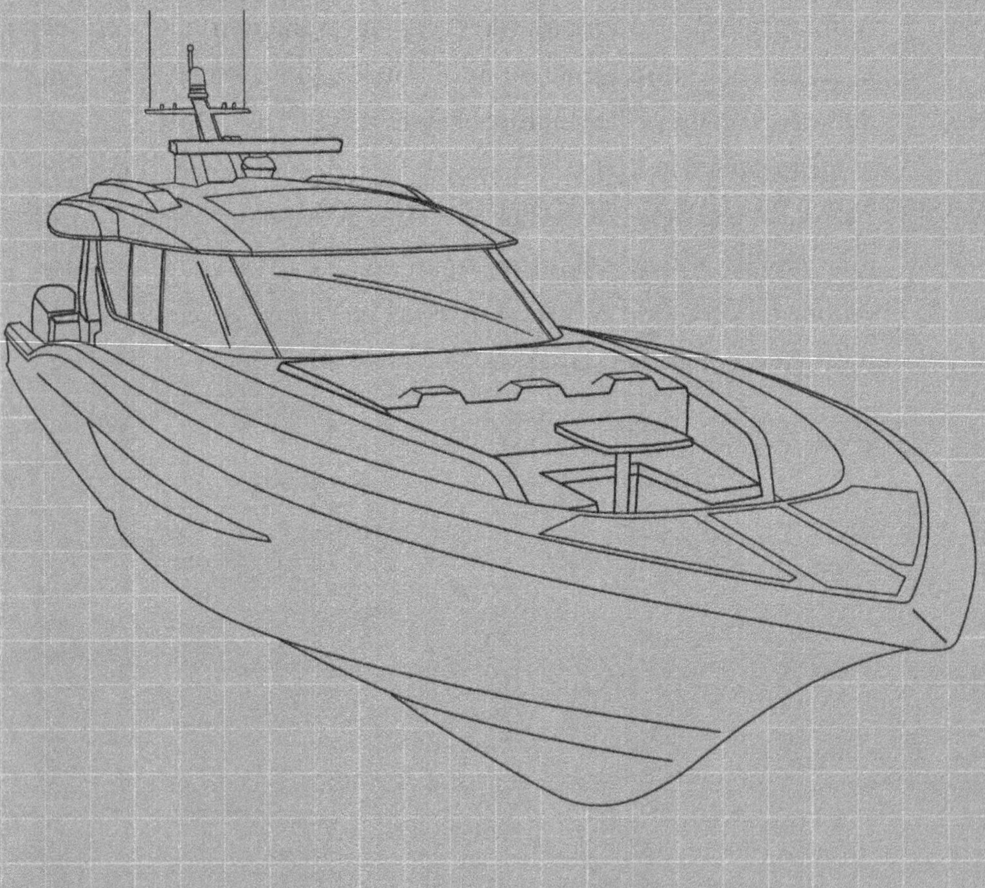

CHAPTER 7

Going International and Digital

A full decade after we gathered the $50,000 I had saved from my night gig repairing bathtubs and the second mortgage we could extract from our home to embark on the crazy adventure of developing a boat company from the ground up, we still employed only eighty-three people and operated out of that one plant—cleverly titled Plant A. In the year 2000, we expanded into what we call Plant B, demonstrating that "thinking outside the box" mentality that fuels all the great innovators. Okay, sarcasm is not my strong suit. The truth is, we reserve our creativity for boats. Calling our plants A, B, C, and D makes it easy for everyone to know where they're going. We'll stick with sensible nomenclature and save our right-brain synapses for developing the kinds of business and manufacturing ideas I am about to describe in this chapter.

In fact, our company has grown at a steady 12 percent annual clip, doubling in size every six years. Doubling when you're small is easy, but once the enterprise reaches a critical mass, it's a whole lot more significant. Just as an illustration, if you start out with twenty-four employees, 12 percent means you bring on three more. At 240 employees, 12 percent growth can mean adding an entire thirty-person department, a qualitatively different proposition.

To give you an idea of how explosive our growth has felt, we hired seventy-nine more employees in 2024 than we had in 2022, net of any departures. We have long since passed the point where I am doing the hiring or meeting every employee, much less knowing everyone's name, their spouse's name, and their kids' names and having a personal connection with them. We have grown to the point where a large number of people in the buildings work in fields I know nothing about and couldn't have envisioned when we were driving home from Atlanta. That is saying a lot considering I learned every aspect of boatbuilding from the ground up, took an interest in the hiring process, always had an eye for marketing, and served as the quarterback of the company's ascension for most of its thirty-five years. Corporate growth is a double-edged sword, but mostly the wonderful artifact of unfathomable success.

One development that has played a small role in our ability to grow into one of the four largest enterprises in the recreational boat segment is our foray into the international market. Or, I should say, the international market's foray into Scout Boats. We didn't purposely build a platform for international sales or develop a sales-and-marketing strategy or supply chain to deliver boats to other countries. It's just that boat people came to us and asked either to sell our boats or buy them. Who says no to that?

The actual mechanics of it started at one of the major boat shows—either Miami or Fort Lauderdale, I forgot which. This was in 2008, when our economy crashed because of the housing bubble that didn't exist in most of Europe. That left the dollar humbled compared to the euro; you could get ten dollars for six euros then. (They're almost on par now.) So international agents came to the boat show and began placing orders because our boats had suddenly become relatively cheap. During the Great Recession, our number one dealer was in Athens, Greece, a city on the Mediterranean in a country that is largely coastline and had an economy that was propped up by constant infusions of debt and a wide divide between rich and poor (sound familiar?). It was great for a while, until that Ponzi scheme came crashing down and Greece essentially went bankrupt.

Selling overseas is different than selling in the US and Canada because they don't really have dealerships in Europe or Australia, or even in Mexico. It's a bit like libraries these days. If you're even half my age, you will remember the days when you went to the public library and it was full of books. You searched the stacks for the book you wanted, and there was a decent chance it would be in the stacks, next to another copy of the same book, because each library stocked half a dozen of the popular titles. But today, most libraries are not repositories of books; they are places you go to pick up books you ordered online two weeks prior. The entire county library system shares a couple of copies of the title you want, and when you place your order, they ship the book from its home library to the library near you. It's a great system for the libraries in an era of budget cuts because they save piles of money on redundant book stocks. It's generally convenient for readers, except it eliminates your ability to walk into the stacks and thumb through books that might interest you. That's exactly how international boat sales work, except we don't charge our customers a quarter if they fail to bring back the boat.

When we sell boats overseas, we don't send an armada of Scouts to, say, Perth, Australia, hoping they will sell and recoup our investment. That would be a ridiculously expensive speculative operation. Instead, a boat broker in Perth contacts us in South Carolina and places an order, remits payment, and gets the boat he or she requested.

We have export dealers in countries around the world, with Mexico and Puerto Rico our two most dynamic, but we have never created an international division or hired an independent sales representative the way some other brands have. This means that most of our exports are the result of two things: relationships we have in the industry or directly with individuals, and the reputation for quality work that dealers want to sell even across the ponds.

As I mentioned, the currency exchange rate no longer favors the US, subtracting 35 to 40 percent of value from our exports. The costs of transporting boats and meeting local regulations in other countries are sufficiently significant that the international trade is sparse. We get custom orders now and then from Scout enthusiasts based elsewhere, but the bulk of our sales are domestic. That may change a bit when we unveil our 670 sports yacht, because high-end vessels like that have such niche markets that every marginal sale makes a big difference.

As you might imagine, we have many customers who are either mega rich or mega famous or both. The one who stands out is the royal family of Qatar, one of the world's richest families.

The royal family of Qatar doesn't exactly purchase our base model 215 Dorado at $77,000 for a spin around the Doha harbor. Because the royal family is attracted to the retro-sleek style of our broken-line hulls, they have ordered five 53-foot boats from us. To meet their custom needs, two of these boats are equipped with six engines on the transom, something you won't see on any other Scout Boat, now or ever. These yachts are plenty wide enough to accommodate all six engines, but the boat must be specially designed with a reinforced transom and some engineering adjustments to make it work. There is no custom-built Scout as custom built as the royal family of Qatar's five Scouts.

Another high-powered customer who stands out in my mind will not be named to protect the hotheaded. Let's just say he's a gazillionaire and a great customer of Scout Boats. He's owned two Scout yachts, a 53-footer and a 42-footer, and he always buys Scouts. I've been to his penthouse, and he considers me a friend. I appreciate him, and our company appreciates his business and will go out of our way to accommodate him, as you're about to see. Some customers exploit this power, which may very well explain their level of success, several standard deviations from the merely rich.

This incident I am about to recount stems from our decision to make feature-rich, digitally operated boats that predict and meet our customers' needs even before they realize they have them—just as car companies installed lane protection and backup cameras and cup holders and intermittent wipers before anyone asked them to. The dashboards that operate all these features are both simpler and vastly more complex than those on simple analog boats, as I'll discuss in much more detail in the next chapter. Bottom line, the more complex the machine, the more different ways it can fail and the more catastrophic the failure because you can't just tighten a bolt with a wrench to remedy the problem.

One day, just as Dianne and I were getting ready to go out to celebrate her birthday, the same thirty-ninth birthday we have been celebrating for four or five years, I got a phone call from this gentleman. (When his number pops up, I take the call, even if I'm running out the door to pay homage to the woman at the center of my world, the mother of my children, the steadfast partner in both my business and my life.) I picked up the phone and was hit with an auditory assault of four-letter words pronounced in rapid succession and at ear-shattering volume. I sensed he might have been ticked off just a tad.

Long story short, one of the three motors on his brand-new Scout Boat blew up off the coast of Nassau, in the Bahamas. That's annoying, it's disappointing, and I can see where it would reduce his enjoyment that day. Furthermore, a guy who spends hundreds of thousands of dollars to have a boat built and delivered expects it to last more than, I don't know, two hours? So, sure, "f" this and "f" that; I get it.

Before he called me, he called the dealer who sold the boat, cussed him up one side and down the other, and threatened him with legal action, and then he called me and did the same, threatening to bury Scout and all our dealers. Okay, I didn't take any of that personally, and the dealer was a big boy who should have been able to manage an irate customer, particularly one who did have some cause to be dissatisfied. It was not the time to mention that we don't create or assemble the engines; that's the work of the good people at the outboard motor company, who have a strong track record, which is why we proudly place their engines on our boats, and if they build a clunker, we are happy to take responsibility for finding a solution even though we did not create the problem. At the same time, we're not Cro-Magnon; we can communicate like adult twenty-first-century humans and work together to solve a problem. Our furious customer is probably adept at problem-solving, given his string of business triumphs.

I told him that if he didn't calm down, I was going to hang up and turn my phone off. "Just listen to me a minute," I said. "I heard what you said; I heard what happened. Let me get into it tomorrow morning." Then I called the dealer, and we commiserated in brotherly unison before I prescribed the workaround. I told him he didn't deserve to be treated that way, and he said the same to me, and we sang Kumbaya in two-part harmony, and then I informed him that I was going to solve the problem by totally throwing the dealer under the bus. This is like the joke about the wife who tells her husband she blames him for something totally out of his control, and he protests that he wasn't responsible. She says, "I didn't say it was your fault; I said I'm blaming you!"

To mollify our customer, someone had to take the blame, and since the outboard motor company was not on the phone calls, I had to blame the dealer. He's a good guy and a valued business partner, and he was smart enough to understand his role in this drama. He agreed to send an apology note while I reached back out to the customer and offered for him to direct all future inquiries directly to me, circumventing the dealer. We had a relationship to salvage, and we couldn't get hung up on the particulars.

Now, he was in the middle of the Caribbean. It would take a month to get another motor to him using traditional routes. Instead, my well-connected customer service people called the outboard motor company and had them airfreight a new motor to the dealer ASAP. The dealer removed the back seat from his private plane and literally flew it, along with a mechanic and all the tools necessary to install it, to the marina in Nassau. Within forty-eight hours, by hook and by crook, the customer's boat was brand spanking new and back on the water, with no one worse for the wear.

We spent a few thousand dollars, the dealer did the same, and we all lived happily ever after. In fact, the next day as I entered the plant, I saw administrative people gawking at this giant tray almost as big as the table itself, scratching their heads and awaiting an explanation and permission to dive in. A big sign was affixed to the tray, which I could now see was covered in baked goods, that said Brownie Points. It's the customer's way of saying thank you, and perhaps "I'm sorry for losing my cool." He and I talked later, and he offered a real apology, noting that twelve family members were with him, and they were just stranded. I waved it off as if it were another day at the office and recalled a lesson I learned early on in my career: You can take bad situations and turn them into good situations by how you handle them.

That dustup behind us, having plumbed the international waters and considered two interesting customers, we turn our attention to the east to mention one other market that might draw future attention. The market every boat maker would like to dip a toe in is China, soon to be the world's leading economy, and with 1.4 billion inhabitants, nine thousand miles of coastline, and twenty million millionaires, a massive market for luxury boats. The Chinese government tightly controls commerce in its country and appears to have little appetite for allowing American boat manufacturers to dominate their industry. Beyond that, where Americans are consumerist spenders, the Chinese are frugal savers. Owning a boat, a nice little luxury in the US, has a different connotation there. For now, as a company that focuses almost exclusively on the domestic US consumer, we have not made any serious forays into China. However, because the only constant in business is change, I wouldn't be shocked to discover that international sales make up a significant percentage of Scout Boats sales twenty years from now.

If you have used a phone, or flown in an airplane, or driven a car no older than Billie Eilish, you have experienced the digital revolution. (Some digital elements in automobiles may go back to Taylor Swift's birth, or even Beyoncé's.) The boat industry, however, was not on board. The conventional wisdom in our industry, to which I heartily subscribed, was KISS—keep it simple, stupid. But in the early 2010s, there was no denying that analog was mostly a vestige of the past and companies that didn't embrace the change were destined to become part of the fossil record, as dead as dinosaurs and woolly mammoths.

The distinction I am making here is in the electrical transmission of information, like a request to lower the anchor or see a depth chart on a screen. Analog signals translate electric pulses of varying amplitude and require miles of wiring to serve as conduit. Analog signals deteriorate with noise and consume copious amounts of electricity. Digital signals translate information via a binary system of zeroes and ones that require almost no wiring, are noise immune, and draw negligible amounts of electricity. Sounds like a no-brainer, right? But wait.

If your speedometer ceases to work while you're shark fishing out at sea, you might be able to jiggle some wires, strip the insulation back and tighten a connection, or jerry-rig it to return to life. It's not brain surgery. When the switch fails in a digital system, it not only transforms multiple systems into expensive metal sculptures, it's also very likely to require a shop with computers and highly skilled engineers to repair. This is my great fear, and a great fear of every boatbuilder, because nothing says irate customer like a day of fishing that turns into a family stranded at sea.

At the same time, we're not inventing new technology here. The entire flight systems in commercial US airplanes and the national air traffic control system at airports employ digital technology, and airplanes are not falling out of the sky. The last major commercial crash (as of this writing, and let's hope as of your reading too) took place in 2001. That's twenty-three years and counting of safe operation. If digital is good enough to put three million people into the sky and bring them safely to earth every day, it's safe enough to use on a recreational marine vessel that goes a tenth the speed, skimming across the surface of the planet.

It wasn't just the advantages discussed above that motivated us to explore going digital: Our boats were becoming increasingly feature rich. Almost anything you could do in your house was becoming possible on the boat. We had so many entertainment systems on the vehicles that they were filling up not just with wires but with screens and buttons and systems. It was becoming complicated and cumbersome to activate many of the features on the boat. It was a bit like visiting a beautiful website full of cutting-edge functionality without a navigation bar at the top or a search feature inside the site. We were offering our customers a wonderful variety of entertainment options, but they were only using a fraction of them because the whole system was becoming ungainly. Digital could solve that by integrating related functions and controlling them with a single switch. For example, suppose you were night riding and you wanted the boat to adjust to that. Let's say that meant starting the water pumps and turning on the navigational lights and a couple of courtesy lights onboard (but not too many or too bright—we wanted to create a mood.) And you wanted to set the musical playlist to romantic evening tunes. All that could be programmed into a single switch called, say "Sunset," and one push of a button on the Garmin screen would engage all your preset choices. All that might have been half a dozen toggle switches you would have had to find and flip in an analog system.

In 2013, we began to realize there was a gaping hole in the industry we could exploit. If we could be first to market with a digital system, we could cement our reputation as the cutting edge of the industry and serve our customers better than literally all our competitors. And we would have a two-year head start on everyone else, who wouldn't know what hit them until part way through our first model year, which would follow a year of research and development. We began working with partners in the digital industry then and unveiled the first digital-built boat in the coastal fishing boat segment. The response was consternation, dismissal, scoffing, and sniggering from everyone within the industry. But not from consumers: They loved it. They had been enjoying the digital world in their homes, with Alexa and smart refrigerators and programmable thermostats and programmable lighting systems. To them, it was the most natural thing in the world. In fact, if consumers gave it any thought, it sounded like this: What took you so long?

There is another group of people who were totally on board: those inside our own plant. Our team is not only used to ongoing change; they expect and revel in it. Innovation is what makes us, us, what keeps us thriving, what underpins the pride we feel for our work. Our staff buys Scout Boat merchandise because they are proud to build the best recreational boats in the world. I don't recall hearing a single negative word from anyone at Scout Boats. But boy, that sure wasn't the reaction from industry insiders.

I'll never forget our press conference at the 2014 Miami Boat Show, where we introduced the first digital Scout. The media were scratching their heads, wondering if we had finally gone off the deep end. Their questions were muted, puzzled, and full of cautionary words. Wasn't this a huge risk? Were consumers ready for this paradigm shift? Would the boat seize up in the middle of the ocean with all these complicated, newfangled apparatuses in it? My answers about airplanes and automobiles and homes and the watch on your wrist didn't seem to mollify them. I took it personally, but I also loved the challenge. It was another opportunity for a high school dropout and his band of misfits from Sa' Ca-a-lina to outsmart the suits in corporate at the multinationals that own our competitors and beat them to the future yet again, and this time, in a fundamental aspect of our industry.

Our competitors did their best to scare and confuse customers, calling our innovation reckless and unreliable. What else could they do? They must have known, deep down in the lower right ventricles of their atrophying hearts, that those plucky independents at Scout had once again beaten them up, taken their lunch money, outfoxed them, and fashioned a superior product. All you had to do was ride in one of our digitally outfitted vessels to understand the new level of convenience that we offered. The express train to the future had left the station and they were still standing on the platform, and they had better catch a Lyft back to the drawing board. Our dealers got spooked after hearing all the propaganda and began lecturing us on all the catastrophic ramifications of our foolhardy move—until the boats began selling.

They weren't entirely wrong, at least not in this sense: The boating environment is not particularly conducive to all the interconnecting signals that operate a functioning digital system. The salt air, the vibrations, the water spray—they're death on these devices. It is a problem we had to solve. Of course, we wouldn't have brought the system to market if we hadn't solved it, which we did by collaborating with a partner in the digital industry to build a boat in a box, which insulates digital systems for usage on the water. There was no point in allowing the revolution to bypass us without taking a swing at a solution. As hockey legend Wayne Gretzky said, you miss 100 percent of the shots you don't take. We took a shot and scored big-time.

Because I pride myself on following the evidence, I don't want to be a Pollyanna about this. The digital solution is a new technology that raised the cost of boats, particularly as they became increasingly customized. Accompanying the digital switches are access to Wi-Fi connections and satellite hookups that require more technology and more cost. We had to build in some analog redundancies for access to some items that owners would not want to be hunting for on the screen. The horn is a good example of that. No one wants to be searching for the horn on the dashboard as another boat is careening toward them threatening a head-on crash. We built in a manual redundancy so the horn can be tooted by hand right above the driver. Additionally, there is a learning curve with all this new technology, as there is with anything new, and that causes some grumbling early on. The more sophisticated the vessels we manufacture, the more sophisticated the operator must be, even as the sophisticated systems we offer make operating the boat easier and more convenient.

We conquered this issue, at least in part, by making the operation simultaneously simpler. The driver can return to the home button on the screen to find a list of options. For example, choosing "circuits" brings up a list of commands that can be indicated manually. And of course, there are all the presets that activate a series of commands with one touch of the screen, as I mentioned previously. All this can be operated through an iPad, for which we have created a docking station inside the boat. The boat can be turned on remotely and commanded to activate select features with the key fob. In short, a Scout Boat is now a lot like a Mercedes automobile in that it puts many more features in the hands of the driver and makes it as simple as possible—once they read the manual and learn a few new tricks.

We were very comfortable being Mercedes, and if the rest of the industry wanted to build Yugos, that was okay with us. (The subcompact Yugo was put out of its misery in 2008.) In fact, though, our competitors quickly emulated us after witnessing the success of our innovations, though I believe we remain ahead of them in this regard a decade later. Even when legacy businesses can't stomach getting a whiff of the future, they are highly motivated by the smell of money and will change when market conditions leave them no other options. We just believe there is never any other option, and that is why we continually funnel investment into our research and development.

Our partner Garmin is working on taking their system cellular, allowing their system to retrieve information via phone and provide bespoke updates on the fly to each individual system. This feature would allow them to develop passive diagnostics and upgrades customized to each boat. The cellular system imposes some limitations on this, but eventually it would pivot to satellites, which offer a level of pinpointing—as you see with your automobile GPS—that is breathtaking and creates a level of functionality not yet available. But it's coming, and we are primed to roll it out first.

With the electric vehicle revolution accelerating upon us, Scout Boat decided we needed to investigate its viability on the water. Again, if the revolution was inevitable, we wanted to be on the leading edge. It is a lesson in understanding that just because you miss 100 percent of the shots you don't take does not mean that you score on 100 percent of your attempts. Quite the contrary, most innovations fizzle on the workbench, but that is the tradeoff we are willing to make to reach market with some cutting-edge idea in every new model. With this in mind, we went about building half a dozen 14-foot prototypes with electric pods on trim tags that were operated with joysticks. This was in the early 2000s, even before Tesla and Rivian and all the electric car manufacturers began transforming the auto industry. At the time we were testing an e-boat, carmakers were still mucking around halfheartedly with electric vehicles, most likely hoping the technology would never prove viable. Now with battery storage technology sufficiently robust, e-cars have grabbed a foothold in the market.

Seeing these developments, we were not going to get Tesla-ed by some boat industry disrupter if we could help it, so we rekindled our efforts to solve the challenges of electric propulsion of boats in 2020. We partnered with a billion-dollar company to build the Zapp, and after a year developed a working model. We established some basic benchmarks for the boat knowing that anything less would render it unpalatable to the boating public. It had to be at least seventeen feet long and accommodate six adults comfortably; it had to run for 2.5 hours on a single charge and reach speeds of 30 miles per hour. And it had to be commercially viable for less than $100,000. Anything less made it a novelty, unworthy of mass production. We weren't interested in selling DeLoreans; we wanted to sell Teslas.

We built a model that exceeded all our parameters, and I ran it up and down the creek behind my house repeatedly. Let me tell you—there is something about flying across the water without any engine noise, the only sound the birds squawking above and the water slapping against the hull. It combined the thrill of power boating with the serenity of sailing, a sublime feeling that I imagine few have experienced. It felt like we were onto something.

And then came the regulators.

If you buy a lamp, it basically must be certified by Underwriters Laboratories (UL) as safe. This tells the consumer that you won't get electrocuted using this lamp unless you chew on the wire insulation while it is plugged in and operated. Absent that designation, not only is the manufacturer liable if anyone gets electrocuted, retail outlets won't go near it, fearing their own liability. Operating an electric charge on the water multiplies the liability tenfold and could put literally our entire operation at risk. For that, we have our own regulatory agency, which ruled that they would not certify anything over 60 volts, no matter how insulated, protected, bubble wrapped, sheathed, enclosed, confined, covered, shielded, padded, and isolated from human contact. For a little frame of reference, a Tesla runs on a 400-volt battery.

Try as we might, we could not summit that limitation, and it put a halt to our efforts. Maximizing the efficiency everywhere, we could push the vessel to 23 miles per hour, 25 percent short of our goal. Running the boat on foils to boost it off the surface of the water, increasing its glide, solved that problem, but that pushed the price over $100,000 and made it impossible to trailer. So, you have this super electric boat, but you can't get it to the dock. We reshaped the boat bottom so that it would plane atop the water from a standing start at 11 miles per hour, from the normal 16 or 17 miles per hour, saving us horsepower and voltage. We even redesigned the running surface to skid across the liquid surface more smoothly, but all our tweaks proved insufficient to make the boat viable at 60 volts. Necessity was the mother of invention, but this necessity was one tough mother. Our e-boat experiment has not come to fruition, but it was a valiant and worthwhile effort, and it was not all for naught.

The little innovations in design and shape were in fact great steps forward in their own right. We are applying some of the principles that the Zapp necessitated to our gas-powered vessels, making them more efficient, smoother riding, and just plain better. As we develop our new 180 model, we are incorporating these advancements. And in the meantime, the Zapp remains on hiatus. Not dead, just in deep sleep. Its time will come.

Next, I get to bang my chest a bit and take a bow for my company's accomplishments, which are, of course, the accomplishments of many hundreds of others as well. As Isaac Newton said, "If I see farther than others, it is by standing on the shoulders of giants."

CHAPTER 8

Entrepreneur of the Year

By the year 2000, we had crossed the one-hundred-employee plateau, at which point I no longer knew everyone by face or name, much less their family situations, life stories, and so on, as I once did. We had grown sufficiently to add Plant B, and my son had begun working with us full time, starting at the bottom and making a few dollars an hour. Scout Boats had crossed the Rubicon again, this time from growing enterprise with a fairly certain future to recognized innovator manufacturing quality and reliability. We had become something, and as the founder and driving force, I had become somebody, at least in the industry. Fame was never my goal—it's not something introverts like me typically seek—and as for fortune, well, my family was already living comfortably, with all the necessities and comforts money could provide. What motivated me then, as now, as at the very beginning, was my mad obsession with building better boats, for winning in the marketplace, for doing right by our growing cadre of employees, and for building a legacy company that could be passed down through the generations of my family.

Building better boats was an ongoing concern, something all of us at Scout Boats dedicated ourselves to every day on the job. Of course, every day on the job meant every day for me, but I have no illusions about all those around me. I'll admit, being so obsessed probably isn't the healthiest thing. A psychiatrist could probably make a whole career out of poking around in the quirky corners of my mind—writing papers, getting a few chuckles, and climbing the professional ladder, all on the back of my boatbuilding fixation.

But I'm at least sane enough to understand and appreciate that it does not afflict everyone else, even those who earn a good living from this enterprise. I don't expect everyone to run and skip to work from the parking lot, but I do expect that they will feel some pride in their work and demonstrate that by their performance. In fact, I'll make the point later that it doesn't afflict my own children, who owe just about everything in their lives to this company, and I am perfectly content with that. Scout Boats only needed one founder team to launch and grow the company, and Dianne and I long ago checked that box.

For me, success in the marketplace is the real prize. It's how I prove to myself and others that I really did have better ideas, something valuable to offer. Growing up around water, I felt I knew something about boats that others didn't. Seafaring coursed through my blood in utero. It got in my hands even before I began picking up scraps at the garage near my house. Over the years it's worked its way into my heart and mind, my soul, and my wallet. Now it's enveloping my family and already showing signs of going two generations deep.

What motivates me about winning, I think, is the same thing that motivates professional gamblers: the need to show the world my prowess, my expertise in this domain. It harkens to my experience at age nineteen when the women at American Fiberglass disdained my expertise because all they could see was a baby face, barely requiring a shave. They doubted my competence; they doubted whether I deserved to be in my position of authority, but I showed them that I did, and that desire—that deep, instinctive, mammalian need to assert my powers—is what I think a psychologist would say motivated me to win. I'm short, not particularly athletic, can't tan to save my life, didn't do well in school even though I have the intellect to do so, and my charm with the ladies has been duly documented in these pages. Winning at boats is the thing I can do, and I wanted to show the world I could. I've never actually spoken, or really thought, those words, but writing a book about your life forces you to dig deep.

Doing right by our employees and striving to build a legacy company have come later, as the company has grown. Right from the beginning we valued the people who worked with us and the enormous contributions they made to company growth with their dedication, hard work, commitment to quality, and increasingly, their subject expertise. By the turn of the millennium, we had become the source of income and benefits for more than a hundred families, and we did not take that responsibility lightly. Despite the ups and downs of the economy, we have never laid off staff.

Legacy building was always in the backs of our minds, at least once survival of the enterprise seemed assured. Dianne and I intended from the start to build a company that would outlive us and provide for our family for as long as possible. I've long admired and studied legacy companies, particularly those with strong brands pungent with the sweet odor of craftsmanship and customer delight, like Mercedes, Harley-Davidson, and Disney. Even our competitor, Boston Whaler, whose venerated founder I recounted meeting in the first chapter and which has manufactured high-quality, luxury coastal fishing boats since I was two years old, has maintained its reputation for excellence and dependability despite its purchase by recreation giant Brunswick in 1996. Back when the aptly named founder Dick Fisher was still at the helm, Boston Whaler advertised their boats' unsinkability by sawing them in half, with Fisher in the bow, towing the stern back to shore. At the time, that was a novel idea. Today it's a sine qua non for boats in our segment of the market.

By 2000, as I was soon to turn fifty and our oldest child was nearing adulthood, I began to turn my attention to the company's long-term prospects. For that I needed a succession plan that would slowly apportion ownership of the company from Dianne and me to our three children, a practice that entails engaging in legal and financial machinations that shield the value of the business from the IRS and direct much of it instead to lawyers.

We've been slowly transferring ownership for years now. We're not done yet, but we've made enough progress that Dianne and I can rest easy knowing our kids will inherit Scout Boats when we're gone. There'll still be some red tape and legal hoops to jump through—probably more than we'd like, but less than if we hadn't planned ahead. And hey, we're hoping our kids will follow our lead when it comes time to pass things on to their own children. The prospect of Scout Boats innovating still and delivering on the same brand promise at the turn of the twenty-second century while under the leadership, or at least ownership, of the blood generations behind us—that thrills me, and I very much hope it comes to pass.

That brings me back to the year 2000, when we'd survived the dreaded Y2K bug that wasn't. We were continuing to grow and feeling our oats; the dark days of the Orlando boat show, Hurricane Hugo, and the 1990 snowstorm were mere dots on the distant horizon, barely visible in the rearview mirror. Our accounting firm at the time nominated me for Ernst & Young's Carolinas Entrepreneur of the Year award, pretty heady stuff for a boat boy working seven days a week gluing fiberglass together with resin to make motorized floatation devices. I knew that winning this award would bring lovely recognition for our company and myself, but the prospect of joining important and impressive winners from across the country and giving a speech was terrifying. Later that year I received a call from my accounting firm informing me that I had worked my way through the levels of triage and was now a finalist for the award, something that elevated both my sense of excitement and trepidation to DEFCON 2. So it was something of a relief when I received the follow-up call sometime later saying I was the runner-up. I could collect my silver medal without making a speech or standing beside bigwigs and famous people for endless photo shoots. Just kidding; there's no hardware for coming in second in this competition. As Dale Earnhardt famously put it, "Second place is just the first loser."[7]

Given that roller-coaster experience and reflecting on consolidation of credit for our collective efforts in one person, the following year I asked our accounting firm to resist nominating me once more, appreciating the sentiment though I did. "Um, Steve," they replied. "That's, uh, going to be a problem." So once again I steeled myself for an honor that I didn't feel I deserved and knew I didn't deserve alone, and this time the phone call from the accounting firm had a much more celebratory tone. I like to frame it this way: On behalf of the outstanding men and women who carried Scout Boats to prominence in the industry, the company's founder was named the 2001 Ernst & Young Carolinas Entrepreneur of the Year. I was thrilled. I was humbled. I was grateful. I was conflicted. And I was going to Palm Springs, California, for the national event, along with Dianne and

---

7 "Dale Earnhardt Quotes," Goodreads, accessed January 3, 2024, https://www.goodreads.com/quotes/109732-second-place-is-just-the-first-loser#:~:text=Quote%20by%20Dale%20Earnhardt%3A%20%E2%80%9CSecond,is%20just%20the%20first%20loser.%E2%80%9D.

our new company vice president, Dave Wallace. We mingled with famous people in business who were leading famous companies, like Microsoft's Bill Gates. NFL Hall of Famer John Elway, fresh off a failed business venture with Michael Jordan and Wayne Gretzky, was the keynote speaker. And here I was, a small boatbuilder from Podunk, South Carolina—the state deemed too small to be a country and too large to be an asylum—rubbing elbows with the rich and famous. And I was the one getting the award.

Inside our eleven-year-old company, it was the Nobel Peace Prize, the MacArthur Fellowship ("genius" grant), and the cover of *People* magazine all rolled into one. Everyone in our shop felt as if they had personally achieved a level of notoriety and recognition, or at least I hoped they did, because we certainly presented it as a company-wide honor that just happened to be bestowed upon me as their representative. It was astonishing to all of us that we were sharing mind space with Microsoft and manufacturing companies many times our size.

Internally, the shine of winning Entrepreneur of the Year wore off pretty fast as we got back to work in the daily combat of manufacturing in a competitive industry. It's not like I put it on my résumé. It's not even like I have a résumé. Who would I give it to? I think I once created a LinkedIn page that says I'm the founder of Scout Boats, and that's it. I'm pretty sure there's no photo. I haven't checked in, well, ever, and I wasn't sufficiently motivated to do so when I began writing this sentence and didn't know the answer. The point is, it was fabulous recognition for the company, and we're very grateful to Ernst & Young and our accounting firm, and after duly celebrating that weekend, we resumed building boats Monday morning at 7:00. But there were real dividends both for me personally and for the company, paid out over the next couple of years.

A few months after the recognition, I was invited to speak to the MBA class at the University of North Carolina in Chapel Hill, about a four-and-a-half-hour drive from my home. On the panel with me were John Belk, who inherited Belk department stores, then the king of retailing in the South, and Steve Hartman, the president and CEO of Industrial Thermo Polymers, inventor of the pool noodle, six to eight million of which were sold annually. It was pretty awe inspiring, and once again I felt out of my league. But it turns out that was a good thing. After all, Steve had essentially won the lottery with his invention, not exactly a viable business plan for MBA students considering their futures. John had won the lottery with his DNA. The students had already missed that … well, boat.

I was the only one of the speakers with whom they could truly identify—a country boy who had stumbled his way to success. I say that with respect for my two panel mates: John ran what was then a $1.3 billion company, or something like that; I have never come close to it and probably never will. (My kids, though, one day …) And we have certainly shopped at his stores, so we have voted with our pocketbooks for his company. Steve turned a novelty idea into a phenomenon and ran a business I don't understand to boot. I give him all the credit in the world for his success. But when it came time for Q&A, the students directed most of their attention to me. They were interested in how to launch a company, scale it, move from laborer to executive, manage growth, juggle your family, and so on. John Belk's expertise in running a top company in his industry might come decades down the road, but I had produced exactly what many of them dreamed of achieving when they graduated.

That discussion sticks in my mind more than two decades later, particularly for a funny moment made possible primarily by John Belk. I spoke to the students about the history of my company—

starting in the garage with my wife, nearly going belly up, remaining debt-free, and so on. John followed and ticked off the same list—nope, did not start the company; nope, never came close to insolvency; nope, my personal fortune was never threatened; oh my god no, we are not debt-free. The students got a good laugh at that, but it did serve to put some distance between these budding entrepreneurs and him and drew them closer to me.

The hits kept coming. In 2023, the marketing guy for Viking Yachts approached me to write a recommendation for Pat Healey, the son of the company founder and a guy I admire very much, for the National Marine Manufacturer Association's Hall of Fame. This is equivalent to the lifetime achievement honor at the Academy Awards for our business, and Pat is richly deserving as the CEO of a $600 million enterprise, about four times our size. I was honored to be asked and penned (metaphorically, of course, I'm no Luddite) a lovely and heartfelt letter extolling Pat's leadership and integrity.

"Um, Steve," said my administrative vice president, Courtney Guice, "that's, uh, going to be a problem."

Okay, it's true, no one actually said those words, either when I asked not to be nominated for Entrepreneur of the Year or when I nominated Pat for the Hall of Fame. I'm busted. The truth is, I can't remember the exact conversations; all I know is that whenever an award is involved, it seems the course of true love never does run smooth, to paraphrase the bard.

Unbeknownst to me but not to Courtney, our PR guy in Orlando, Mark Jerkins, had assembled a three-minute video nominating me for the very same Hall of Fame. "No problem," I probably didn't say, but it captures the essence of my response, because I had no chance against Pat, particularly inasmuch as I had seconded his nomination.

I relegated the matter to the place in my mind where I store random trivia, like Ed Marinaro's career rushing yards at Cornell (4,715 yards and 50 touchdowns on 918 carries) or Dick Bertram's birthday (February 4, 1916, which would have put him at about fifty when I met him as a teenager) and moved on to other things, most notably a meeting of our internal insurance company in Switzerland. And it was there that I received a phone call from Washington, DC. The number looked vaguely familiar, which of course it should, because I have been an active member of the National Marine Manufacturer Association for years. They were on the phone with truly exciting news, that I was to be inducted into their Hall of Fame.

This is not like winning an award; this is the Hall of Fame in the association representing the thing I have literally done since the age of fourteen. Besides eat, breathe, sleep, brush my teeth, wear clothes, and speak when spoken to, I can't think of any other activity I have done continually since the age of fourteen besides build boats, and here I was going into the boatbuilding Hall of Fame. This must have been what it felt like for some not quite immortal to enter the Hall of Fame with the likes of Babe Ruth, Willie Mays, and Ken Griffey Jr. The class of 2024 is Mark Schwabero and me;[8] he's the former chairman and chief executive officer of Brunswick Corporation, having previously served as president of Mercury Marine. We joined the likes of Ole Evinrude of Evinrude engines; Bill Healey, Pat's father and the cofounder of Viking Yachts with his brother Bob; the aforementioned Dick Fisher and Dick Bertram, the two men who made my jaw drop in the Outboard Shop; and Johnny Morris of Bass Pro Shops. It is hard to convey what an enormous honor this was for me, a simple-

---

8 "Hall of Fame Award," National Marine Manufacturers Association, accessed December 16, 2024, https://www.nmma.org/industry-awards/hall-of-fame-award.

minded kid living a dream of mixing liquid with fabric and making something that floats.

Truly, the NMMA Hall of Fame is a transcendent honor, which I thought about every moment for months leading up to the event and for weeks beyond that, but I'm starting to find myself on the mountaintop struggling to breathe in the thin air. I have imposter's syndrome—that feeling that I'm a fraud and don't deserve to be considered with the giants of the industry. I'm very proud of what we've built and would stack up Scout's boats against anyone else's. I think we have an amazing team that has grown us through both calm and troubled waters, and I enjoy a firm belief that our future is greater still, irrespective of my gradual departure from the company. I'm not falsely modest about our success; it's just that I recognize how much of our success is timing, luck, great people around me, and the support of my wife and family. Consequently, I said not one word about this honor to anyone. I keep waiting for the very regretful email informing me that it was a very unfortunate mix-up, and they meant to induct Pat but saw my name on the letter of recommendation and accidentally entered it into the database. (I'm fairly sure Pat will get his turn next year.)

The problem is my proud wife blabbed about it to everyone she saw: her friends, family, hair stylist, auto mechanic, Uber driver, waiter, and random individuals on the street. I'm hoping the hubbub will die down soon and we can get on with the daily business at hand, but I will carry that Hall of Fame designation in my heart and remind myself every day that I am, at Scout Boats, a bar or two in a symphony of accomplishment with more notes than anyone else, but still, nowhere near even a majority of the composition.

The metaphor is apt because Beethoven, generally considered the greatest composer of symphonies, agonized over every note, tearing up pages of composition and regretting bars of music long after they had been published, performed, and acclaimed. We all make mistakes, and I have made my share, but I've always made sure to learn from my mistakes and the mistakes of others and move forward. One mistake I made repeatedly during much of my career was to overreact emotionally to every challenge and setback we encountered, no matter how microscopic in retrospect. I would never verbally belittle anyone, but nonverbal displeasure speaks volumes as well, and I was guilty of displaying that. I would throw my safety glasses and storm off or put up some other fuss every time something went awry, and it became something of a joke among some of the staff that the boss was a bit of a hothead. It was in that vein that one of my colleagues at Scout bought me a Tasmanian Devil action figure, which I accepted with bemused gratitude and displayed prominently on my desk. The message was a punch with a velvet fist, and I took note. If the staff is laughing about the boss's inability to control himself, maybe he's not the leader he thinks he is. That toy was a daily reminder that I needed to grow up, control my temper, and lead calmly. I would resolve instead to stew over the problem when I went home, by which time it had already been solved, but if not, the emotional hurricane had passed. In either case, it was easy to see just a few hours later how inconsequential the issue had been in retrospect. My blood pressure and I are happy to report that I've been much calmer and less flappable for the last decade or so, and I haven't looked at the Tasmanian Devil in years.

Inherent in writing a book, particularly one with a whiff of memoir like this one, is the sense of completion. An athlete writes his or her book after their athletic exploits have ended. Presidents write their memoirs after their terms in office. Business leaders retire and then tell their tales. In each case, the doing is done, and they are on to a next chapter of life. There is some of that for me. I have relinquished the role of president of the company and have been spending as much time traveling for pleasure as working recently. But the gears have not stopped turning, and we are embarking on some very exciting innovations at Scout Boats that continue to stoke my fire and reinforce my belief that the company is headed in the right direction with the throttle pushed fully open.

For one thing, we're halfway through a $3 million office renovation as I write this. It's not a vanity project. Our offices are twenty years old in 2024 and have become dated, which is something of a business problem when you consider that 80 to 90 percent of the people who buy our boats visit our factory. Additionally, I learned from Garmin's facility when I visited it in Kansas—they're the $8 billion world leader in avionics—that the latest studies of human behavior among millennials and Gen Zers indicate that work-life balance is a crucial selling point for businesses today when recruiting staff. What do I know about work-life balance? Work is my life, and my life has been my work. Building boats, riding on boats, racing boats—that's ambrosia for me. Even if being an accountant or a Harley dealer or an engineer at Boeing were my vocation, boats would be my vacation, the activity you would find me engaged in all weekend. When I'm building boats, what do I need a break for? If I had a break, I'd be building boats!

The five hundred people I work with, on the other hand, require incentives to apply themselves for hours on end at the glorious task of boatbuilding, incentives besides a paycheck; generous health, dental; and 401(k) benefits; and time off for other activities. At Garmin, I saw a whole suite of leisure and recreation facilities—a basketball court, a food court, and more. We're building a 250-seat cafeteria, cornhole setups, and an outdoor patio with fans so employees and visitors can sit outside while they eat. I thought my company owned a factory, but it is turning into a community center, which apparently is the investment required to keep the operation humming along.

As I write this, we are repurposing some of the lessons learned from our collaboration with the emir on his massive boat to produce the largest production boat powered by outboard motors ever made—a 67-footer with five 600-horsepower engines on the back that is once again causing tremors in our industry. *Motorboat & Yachting* magazine called it a "lean, mean 3,000-horsepower speed machine" that hits 60 miles per hour and has a range of five hundred miles.[9]

At seventy thousand pounds of carbon-fiber epoxy, the 67LXS offers the luxury of a yacht, with three staterooms, a theater room, and entertainment package, but with some very significant advantages. Boats with inboard motors require at least six feet of water to get moving, which is why owners also buy tenders to bring them to and from shore. Our 67-footer will operate in thirty-six inches of water, allowing its owners to enjoy all the luxurious living that yacht owners do but also pull up to a dockside restaurant or come ashore for a beach day. The owner of this boat can fish in the ocean by day and kick back on the beach at night nursing a beer and watching the sun set. On top of that, if ever the words *sleek* and *sexy* can be attributed to a boat, the 67LXS is the one. Shaped like a teardrop designed to win a knife fight, the 67LXS will cut through water like a hot blade through pudding.

We view this as a long-term investment in the Scout brand and an opportunity to own a segment of the boat-owner market that our competitors haven't even discovered. And it's not the only bright idea on the drawing board. We're also recycling the hull-design lessons of our jettisoned electric vehicle project to build an 18-footer that can plane up faster than anything on the market today. The point is that

9 Howard Walker, "Scout 67 LX First Look," Motorboat & Yachting, February 9, 2023, https://www.mby.com/news/scout-67-lx-125043.

Scout Boats isn't over; it's just getting started, and my role, though diminished, remains robust. Creating something in the marketplace that doesn't exist continues to … float my boat.

As we motor into the second quarter of the twenty-first century, Scout Boats has charted a new course to success: selling fewer boats but at premium prices. We're taking a page from Viking Yachts' playbook—they're raking in $600 million a year, selling just seventy-five sport fishers at an average of $8 million apiece. Now, we're not quite in yacht territory—our sport boats are a different product. But we do see the vector of the industry, and we're riding that wave.

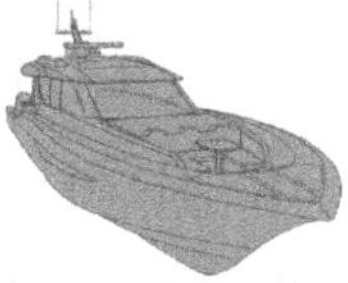

CHAPTER 9

Considering the Future

All my thoughts about boatbuilding today are firmly fixed upon the future of the industry and our company, and my family's role in both. COVID provided a tidal wave of demand to our industry that hasn't ebbed, and we are optimistic about what lies ahead. Four brands dominate the luxury coastal fishing boat market: Brunswick's Boston Whaler, Grady-White, us, and Pursuit, in that order, sell 80 percent of the boats in our segment of the market. Boston Whaler is a legacy company with a sterling reputation and the marketing muscle of a big corporation behind it. Grady-White produces beautiful, high-quality boats. We're the innovator in the industry, and Pursuit does a good job balancing comfort and fishing. None of us are going anywhere unless independently owned Grady-White sells out to a corporate overlord that destroys the brand. I'm confident that our obsession with innovating and staying true to our brand promise of quality, reliability, sleek design, and cutting-edge features will continue to carry us forward.

There is one other element of our company that gives me buoyancy about the future, and that is the first-rate people we have surrounded ourselves with. Again, this isn't false modesty: I personally chose many of these people, and a few others who happen to be my children and raised by my values. All of them have in common a dedication to company principles like hard work without excuses and customer service without exception. As I shift into semiretirement and ultimately into retirement, these people are the future of the company and deserve some recognition.

I can't name all five hundred employees—heck, I don't even know most of them—but I can tell you that we hire for the qualities I described. Those who stick around exemplify them. We know that they take pride in their work because we sell our merchandise at cost to our employees, and they gobble up every new design. It is very gratifying to see people around town wearing branded Scout Boats hats, T-shirts, and other merch, so when I say our team wears their pride on their sleeves, I mean that literally as well as figuratively. In the interest of space, I'd like to focus on a handful of essential team members who have distinguished themselves and have been critical to our ongoing success. First on the list is our president, Dave Wallace.

Dave started as our sales rep for the Great Lakes region and was selling Scout boats in Ohio, Michigan, Wisconsin, Indiana, and Illinois; and he was doing a great job when things began to fall apart with our then-VP of operations. Those kinds of situations are always uncomfortable because we knew we would have to make a difficult change and then go find someone else using a process that had just failed. When you hire someone for an executive position, you think you've got the best candidate. When it turns out they're not a good fit, it's demoralizing and starts the dispiriting process all over again. Just when I was drawing in my breath to prepare for another search, I traveled with Dave for a week around the Great Lakes. I recognized some qualities I did not know he possessed and started dialogue with him to become our vice president of operations. I realized his prior experience working in manufacturing for a major aerospace company along with his sales experience would serve us well. Dave personifies the values of our company and had an added skill that turned out to be critical for success in the job and continues today to serve us well: He understands market conditions for pricing products.

Ordinarily, when we build a boat, we price it at whatever it costs and then add a predetermined margin. But Dave understood early on that the margins could vary based on a variety of factors, most significantly the distinctiveness of the boat. Unlike our competitors, we regularly unveil new and unique features that transform the seafaring experience. For a time, our offerings stand unmatched in the market. We introduce unique features and experiences that aren't available elsewhere—at least until competitors replicate them in the following model year. This means that customers seeking these innovative elements have only one choice: Scout Boats. For that we could charge a premium above the standard margin. The risk is that if you price your product too high for the marketplace, buyers will turn their noses up at the minor upgrade you're so proud of and head for your competition. It takes a real feel for the marketplace to make these pricing decisions. Dave is a master at that.

Dave also has an unshakeable belief in the Scout brand. As I mentioned, I am a student of branding and believe strongly in the power of a nameplate. We know that putting a "swoosh" on a sneaker adds twenty bucks or more to its value in the marketplace because the Nike brand is so powerful and conveys many positive attributes to the buyer. We see the same thing in my part of the country with Publix Super Markets, which charges a bit more for groceries than stores that sell on price but always offers a stellar shopping experience. Rolex watches, Lexus automobiles, Shimano bicycle supplies, Apple, and Amazon are all examples of amazing brands whose names convey added value. When the person running your sales department is a brand ambassador, a natural cheerleader for the products and the company behind them, you have a hand-in-glove fit. In Dave's case, it meant our pricing was more aggressive than I was sometimes comfortable with. There have been instances when Dave has advocated for a price tag that shocked me, but he's right way more often than he's wrong, and I bow to his expertise.

Over the twenty-five years he's been with us, Dave has been an invaluable asset to the company and has risen through the ranks to the position of president. As I've stepped away from daily duties and focused entirely on the company's vision, he has filled that gap admirably. Among his many contributions, Dave is a tough and skilled negotiator, which has served us well on numerous occasions, as you can imagine. It was a formidable adversary when we had to negotiate his compensation package, which is based on a percentage of sales and profit, but it's perfect for his personality. He is naturally driven to grow the company first as a matter of pride, but as the basis for his compensation, he has extra motivation to keep his foot on the accelerator. In that way, he and I are a perfect match: He has his eye on sales and profit numbers every quarter while I'm studying the horizon, three to five years ahead.

That said, there are situations where the two perspectives clash. For example, most of our growth has been in larger, more expensive boats bought by people who are less price sensitive. I have had to reign Dave in on pricing our entry-level boats because the market for $50,000 boats is much more price elastic, and we need to be careful not to price ourselves out of that market. With all the profit in the higher end of the market, Dave's focus is firmly fixed there, and understandably the bottom of our market hardly commands any of his attention. For me, the long-term viability of the operation is paramount, and I'm concerned about losing brand strength at the bottom of the segment and disadvantaging us when those buyers move up. A customer with a good Scout Boats experience, no matter how much they paid, might be a Scout buyer for life. Yet, our brand equity will be zero for someone who passes on a Scout because we were overpriced when they were purchasing at the lower end of the market. This is an area of—maybe not quite tension—but discussion and accommodation between us. When the individuals involved respect each other and recognize that they're all on the same team, these differences are more a matter of exploration than a clash of opinions.

Because Dave is merely the president, I can sometimes get my way when we disagree. But with Courtney Guice, our executive vice president of administrative services, it's a different story. Courtney is my indispensable right hand. Courtney tells Dave and me where to be, what to say, and whom to meet. She handles our calendars and intercepts problems before they make their way to the C-suite. Courtney began as a production employee twenty years ago and has proved her mettle ever since.

In fact, we hired Courtney as a teenager, and upon earning her accounting degree, she was prepared to leave Scout Boats and launch her career. It was Dave who recognized her potential and offered her a promotion to sales coordinator. That kept her around long enough to showcase her world-class multitasking skills, which earned her more and more responsibilities. I believe somewhere in her job description it includes the phrase "power behind the throne," but in reality, she's more like the "knower of all things Scout." She has her hands in every aspect of the business and may know more about the company's history, operations, and day-to-day activities than anyone else. She also handles all my non-Scout businesses, which means not only could Scout not function without her, but neither could I personally.

I should never have begun doing business with Helen Pratt-Thomas, our company's banker, my wealth manager, and the coordinator of my advisory committee, which does all our succession planning. Even once I hired her, I shouldn't have continued. And when she switched banks, I should have waved goodbye and remained with the only bank I had ever done business with. The issue is, she is so damn competent.

In the 1990s, following Wachovia Bank's acquisition of my local bank, the only one I'd ever done business with since I began stashing my extra nickels in an account as a teenager, I went in for the first time to ask for a $100,000 line of credit. At the time, Scout was a debt-free $10 million operation, or something like that, with more than $100,000 in their bank. It turns out that Wachovia was happy to have my money, just not to share it with me. Worse, they slow-walked the whole rejection process. The loan officer I talked with steered our conversations left and right and dragged it on for weeks before finally sending me out empty handed.

A year or two later, Helen called me and asked for a meeting to see what she could do for us. When she walked in with the same guy who had disrespected me, I politely sent them packing. But she called again, apologized, explained the internal issues Wachovia was having—a couple of years later, on the verge of going belly up, they were gobbled up by Wells Fargo—and promised to leave the guy behind. We began talking with Helen and realized that she was a bulldog who simply got things done. I'm not the easiest customer because I'm still the son of a navy guy who wants everything perfect and at the lowest cost, but Helen has helped us make good decisions along the way.

I'll never forget when we established a complex side business funded by a 7.65 percent loan in the early 2000s when interest rates had gone haywire. It was a good deal until it wasn't, as interest rates plummeted. The penalty for trading down to a lower-cost loan was substantial, but Helen helped us restructure it and extract ourselves from that high rate. A couple of years later, when she bolted Wells Fargo for South State Bank, we went with her, and we're glad we did.

Around the same time we began working with Helen, Carol Givler joined our company as controller. A retired air force officer, she had worked as an auditor at the big four accounting firm Ernst & Young when Dianne found her. At the time, we were about a $15 million company with sixty-five or seventy employees, every one of whom I knew personally. Carol whipped our accounting processes into place and ran the accounting department through all the ebbs and flows of our company. Now it's ten times the size and complexity, and, until recently, we have not had a chief financial officer. With a controller who accounts for literally every penny, it hasn't seemed necessary until just recently. That is quite unusual for a business our size, and it's a testament to Carol.

If you saw Carol's desk, you would think you had gone back in time. She is an old-school accountant who kills more trees than Japanese beetles do, but if you asked her for a piece of information, she would peer above the piles of paper before her and slap the exact document into your hand. Carol is so diligent that one time I pulled a Scout T-shirt from the shelf, and she asked me if I wanted to pay her cash or have her payroll deduct the $19.99 I owed. She's one of the four or five spokes of the Scout Boat wheel, and I don't know what we would do without her.

Alan Lang grew up with my son, Stevie, and started at Scout right out of college in 1998 in the options department. From the plant floor, his gift of gab got him moved to sales. It was from there that his fists almost got him cut loose.

Alan was a college wrestler at Cumberland College who was living the wild life in his early adult days. He would come to work with a black eye now and then from a bar or street fight precipitated by some verbal spat. One Monday he showed up with rumors swirling around him that he had knocked a guy out at the Coastal Carolina Fair and had to dodge the police to get home. At that point, I pulled him aside and told him that he did a great job representing our company while at work and needed to do a better job of it on his off hours. Of course, that was the least of the problem, but I knew it would resonate with him because he was such a dedicated member of the team.

Alan doesn't fight people anymore; in fact, he is the company's most articulate representative of the Scout brand. When we debut a new model, it isn't Dave or me whom we tap to tell its story in videos and sales meetings with dealers. It's Alan. Now he's our director of sales and marketing, and people buy our boats in part because they know they can trust him. It's nice to see a young man you watched grow up come on board, grow up some more, and thrive.

My daughters have brought several multiples of good fortune to our company and lives by growing into exceptional young women who make their parents proud every day, marrying men of such fine quality that they have managed to deserve our daughters, bestowing upon us grandchildren, and bringing those talented spouses into the business. For neither son-in-law was this inevitable. And each understood that he must start at the bottom at Scout Boats, or at least the bottom as befit the skills they brought with them.

Brandon Dalton married our youngest child, Stephanie, in 2015 and came aboard immediately. It was mere coincidence that he is as obsessed with boats as his father-in-law, but he has made himself indispensable to our operation. A physically intimidating guy, Brandon has the teddy bear personality to manage other people and interact with clients. Lo and behold, those have been his two functions at Scout Boats.

The grandson of a manufacturing company CEO, Brandon brought leadership skills to our operation and made his way to supervisor of our Plant D, where we manufacture our largest and most sophisticated boats. Fully bought in to our 5S lean manufacturing approach in which we measure everything and then strive for greater efficiency and quality, Brandon also displayed the soft skills to keep employees engaged and proud of their work. After a while, it became clear that we needed his soft skills on the client side more than inside, and so we moved him to customer service, where he became the go-to guy for all technical questions about the electronics and other expensive components on our most luxurious boats. Capitalizing on his specialized knowledge, we designated him our sole tech representative whose job is entirely composed of collaborating with dealers and working with individual owners to short-circuit problems that may arise. Brandon has contributed immeasurably to the Scout Boats reputation for quality and exquisite service.

Our first son-in-law is William Ferguson, the son of teachers from South Carolina horse country, the little town of Kershaw, South Carolina. William met our middle child, Sherrie, when they were both undergraduates at Clemson University, where he majored in packaging engineering before interning with Kraft Foods. William joined Scout's engineering department in 2003 and brought three invaluable qualities to the business: an intellectual's commitment to our best ideas, like our 5S manufacturing program; a big heart for everyone around him; and a sly sense of humor.

When Sherrie first brought William home to meet Dianne and me, we of course made an effort to get to know him. Among the many legitimate questions was one off-the-wall salvo fired by Dianne about a topic with which she was not well-versed: the use of marijuana among college students. Rare is the young man away at college, whether in my time or in my children's, who has not at least experimented with a toke on a joint or a hit on a bong at some frat party or postvictory football celebration. Certainly, we didn't want our daughters marrying potheads, but the question of whether they had smoked a doobie now and then during their ascent into adulthood never occurred to me. Evidently it did to Dianne.

"Have you ever been on the pot?" was the way she put it, which gave William time to divert attention away from Dianne's query and into the meaning behind the question at hand.

Scrunching up his face in mock confusion, he retorted, "What do you mean?" Then there ensued such a convoluted discussion of the meaning of being "on the pot," with all its tributaries and arteries, that the conversation steered so far astray that he never had to answer a question he most certainly did not want to subject himself to upon first meeting his girlfriend's parents. Since then, "What do you mean" has been William's signature retreat from any uncomfortable conversation and a source of shared family humor.

I'm glad to say he has gotten off the pot enough to work his way up the ladder to vice president of manufacturing at Scout Boats. As you can imagine, this is a critical post at a company that … manufactures. The most intellectual person in the plant, William directs his staff to read a selected business book each month and report on what they've learned. For that and myriad other reasons, we have a remarkably cohesive and disciplined team producing the best boats in the world.

And two valuable sons-in-law.

Finally, there is our social director, also known as my sister-in-law, Donna. My wife's sister, Donna is officially our fleet manager, a big enough job in itself. But her main role, if you asked our employees, is unofficial event planner. If there is a Halloween event to be planned, or a Christmas party, or baby shower, or anything else that brings the staff together and spreads good cheer, Donna is the ringleader, spreading good cheer. Donna is family, and a thirty-year employee of Scout Boats, but she is also a dear friend.

I covered my wife's role in the founding of the company and will merely mention here that without Dianne Potts there would be no Scout Boats, period. She moved on from working for the company eventually and has played the role of wife, mother, and chief cheerleader since. My three children have been indispensable to the recent success of the operation, particularly my son, Stevie, who has worked with us the longest and has found his niche in research and development, the area of our company that makes Scout Boats special. Among the things I admire about Stevie is that he knows his strengths and leans in on those and has no desire to be the boss when he can instead have an exciting, challenging, and fulfilling job doing what he's superb at.

Sherrie and Stephanie are smart and talented and great at running the parts of the company currently under their purviews. Both of them started at Scout Boats in entry-level roles making the same pay as everyone around them, and both rose to their current positions—running the HR and finance departments respectively—on merit. In addition, Sherrie's husband, our son-in-law, runs the manufacturing operation as our director of facilities, and again, is masterful at his job, as anyone can see when they look at one of our boats and consider our reputation for quality and reliability. I am extremely proud of my girls and grateful to have their talents propelling the company forward. They don't see it, but they have the best positions in the company because they have jobs and significant ownership, and at the end of a long week of work can go home to their families and detach from the daily grind. As part owners of a successful business, they can travel as they please to exotic locales, eat at fancy restaurants, provide their children with all the material advantages to succeed in life, and have, as Stephanie says, "yachts of fun" with the grandparents. They don't have to eat, sleep, and breathe Scout Boats, at least not 24/7, or shoulder the blame for everything that might go wrong. I have exported those burdens to Dave Wallace, and though he is compensated robustly for that responsibility, it is not conducive to the easy life.

Leaving my children in their roles and passing the helm to Dave is the best decision for Scout Boats and all the individuals involved, but family-owned companies are a combination of financial asset and emotional vessel. My daughters may feel disrespected, passed over for the top job as if I'm questioning their competence, when in fact I am protecting their way of life. If any other employee in the company feels undervalued, they might grumble to their colleagues or leave the business altogether, but when the one-third owners are dissatisfied, Dad hears it at the dinner table and must deal with his own swirl of emotions involving the sad faces on his little girls. I guess no matter the age of your children, sometimes Dad just has to make the right decision, whether they appreciate it at the time or not. I know that as the company becomes increasingly profitable and valuable, my kids will thank me (silently, I'm sure) for sparing them boatloads of work as their net worth expands.

Over the past few years, Dianne and I have more thoroughly enjoyed the fruits of our labor, particularly engaged in two pursuits—luxuriating aboard boats and traveling. We have had the great fortune of seeing most, if not all, of the seven modern wonders of the world and have visited dozens of countries near and far. Viewing the wondrous geography and built environments of other worlds, hearing different languages and perspectives, meeting different peoples of all types, participating in their cultures and eating their foods, and most of all learning about their histories, is both joyous and mind expanding and has further convinced me that we are one human family, despite our insignificant differences. Each of us has the common desire to give our children better lives than we have had. There are two ironies in this. First, I never liked history in school, as it was reduced to dry facts and poured into our heads with the expectation that it would be excreted onto a page come test time. But now learning world history on-site might be my primary indulgence. The second irony is that almost none of the places that beckon us to return repeatedly are reachable by a Scout Boat. Our boats are made for coastal recreation with the travel range limited by the gas engine on the back. They can't cross the seven seas—or even half of one. No boat can be everything, and that is what ours are not. But fortunately, someone else manufactures and operates airplanes.

Here's another irony of my life. I am less formally educated than almost everyone else in my position and almost everyone in an administrative position in my own company. The schoolhouse was not for me. And yet, one of the ingredients of my secret sauce has been my drive to remain a student every day of my life. I am always eager to learn something from whomever will teach me, no matter their station in life, or even from no one but the ill winds of bad experiences. I started this company with an expertise in only two things—building a simple boat and managing a department. I haven't run any departments in years and wouldn't be able to make a single sale if I were still peddling the boats we offered in 1990. I've learned about electronics and design and marketing and branding and all the many annoying necessities of running a business, like permitting, insurance, legal, and so on since then, and not a day goes by when

I don't make a very intentional effort to learn something I didn't know. As I mentioned, much of the inspiration for our office upgrade came from a fact-finding visit to the US headquarters of our partners at Garmin, who manufacture the digital communication tools on our boats. That mission to Kansas was entirely a matter of gleaning insights into enterprise dynamics and how the built environment can foster community and engagement inside the workplace—a sentence I could not have uttered three words of ten years ago.

I mentioned that always learning was one of my keys to success; the other is the recognition, which I have referred to here repeatedly, that everything in life is a team sport and requires others to win. I take the lion's share of the external credit for Scout Boats' success, and I'm not too humble to acknowledge that is appropriate, as the founder, driving force, chief decision-maker, and owner of the enterprise. But there is no such thing as a singular success. No such thing. Even a tennis player, who wins and loses by his or her own play on the court, or a boxer, who stares down an opponent with bad intent alone in the ring, has a team behind them. A trainer, nutritionist, exercise physiologist, manager and coach, publicist and lawyer—all of them support the performer and can affect their performance. Jerry Seinfeld needed the actors playing Kramer, Elaine, and George Costanza, not to mention Larry David and the writers, a supportive network, and stalwart production team. And I am not engaged in nearly as solitary an effort as they were. Even at the very start, when Scout Boats wasn't even yet that, when all the plans for the company were in my head, I required the aid and encouragement of a spouse and an employee, and our need for outside assistance ballooned quickly after that. I can't remember, much less thank, all those whose contributions great and small shaped the living entity that this operation is today. Recognizing that early on served as a catalyst for me to treat everyone in the shop as kings and queens, and to demand that they treat each other similarly.

I wouldn't call it a key to success, but I need to acknowledge that the start-up that Dianne and I birthed decades ago would simply not have been possible today, at least not the way we went about it. Before we had anything else, we had timing on our side. Melding an idea with fiberglass and resin, forged by elbow grease and lubricated by optimism, we formed a company with products to sell that the consumer wanted to buy, jump-started by a $50,000 investment. That put us in a warehouse and carried us for a year, funding our attendance at the Atlanta show with a tractor-trailer full of boats. The inflation-adjusted 2024 amount of $127,000 would have gotten us exactly bubkes today. Squat. Nada, nil, and zilch. Opening the doors of the warehouse alone would eat up that sum and more, with all the environmental permits, Title 5 hazardous waste regulations, legal and environmental requirements, and probably a costly site remediation. That doesn't account for time: It would have taken two years before we could have even bought our first roll of fiberglass. If you want to know why there are so few independent boat manufacturers today, start there. The $1 million start-up costs and long lead-up times sideline the small operators and pave the way for conglomerates to dominate the industry. And that might be understating the amount required. It might be a million five. It's also not the only reason that independents are selling out to the corporate behemoths. Economies of scale have catapulted every industry, not just boat manufacturing, toward consolidation. Had we faced such daunting headwinds when contemplating our own entry into this business, I doubt you would be reading this book.

We didn't have a million dollars, or $394,000 in 1989 money, and wouldn't have been willing to lay out that kind of currency to lawyers and engineers without any guarantee of getting to the starting line. Besides all the other factors that led to our success, the calendar played a role. Once again, though I am proud of my own hand in the business's success, I'm keenly aware and appreciative of the tailwinds that pushed us in the right direction for which I not only can take no credit but was lucky to have behind me.

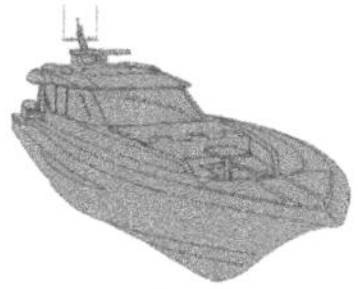

CONCLUSION

Paying Off My Dad

My dad was a military man, for better and worse. The downside was that he was at sea half the year, and that left me to raise myself to some degree. Being the son of a father who is away for six months is tough, and I often missed having a father at home, but the upside was that it also forced me to grow up and figure things out for myself at a young age. It was a mixed blessing when my dad was home, too, because he was demanding and aloof and sometimes treated me as if he was my commanding officer. That instilled in me the importance of discipline and hard work, two qualities that have been critical to my success as an adult. When I was thirteen, this duality struck home after a particular experience that led me to both loathe and appreciate my father—more of the former at that tender age and more of the latter as I became an adult.

Being a military father, he had exacting standards and wanted everything to be just as he expected, like the spit polish on his black patent leather dress shoes. Under his discerning eyes, I was assigned a series of chores and was expected to do them and do them correctly—no, perfectly. This was not in exchange for any incentive or payment—I didn't receive an allowance of any kind—it was merely how I earned by keep, my payment for room and board.

One of my main chores was to wash and detail my dad's prized Pontiac Bonneville every Saturday morning. The Bonneville, named for the salt flats in Utah where early car races took place, was a full-size, high-performance, fuel-injected vehicle with distinctive protruding grille that was manufactured from 1957 to 1981 and aimed at biting off a piece of Cadillac's stronghold with a lower price tag. The Bonneville was relaunched later, but its heyday had passed. Many of its models came standard with features that were unusual in the early 1960s, like power windows, steering, and brakes and the coolest, newest thing—a patented Hydra-Matic automatic transmission. For a man on a military salary, it was a stretch to purchase at $3,500 new but was the doorway to luxury that eluded our family in most other aspects of life. My dad loved cars and boats and passed that on to me, so that rumbling behemoth was a love of both our lives. And because I always worked hard to earn my father's approval, I took to the task of washing the car with particular pride and gusto, hoping to bask in the glow of that gleaming beauty together with my dad. I cleaned every nook and cranny of that automobile, including the whitewall tires, the headlights, and the metal trim where the doors met the undercarriage. I could just hear the compliment my father would bestow upon me.

Early one Saturday morning, two of my best friends rode up to our driveway on their bikes and waited for me to finish because we had planned to go fishing. If you were to make a pie chart of my nonschool activities at age thirteen, fishing would have represented a fat slice. When I hurried to finish my chore and told my dad that I was done, he came out to the driveway, sauntered around the car with furrowing brow, stopped, then circumnavigated it again, sneered, and walked away, grumbling that I wasn't done. Crestfallen because of the hard work I had put into it despite my eagerness to complete the chore and ride away, I asked him what was wrong. "You figure it out," he said and ambled back into the house, shaking his head in disgust.

Imagine being a thirteen-year-old waiting for your friend to complete a chore so you could all engage in your favorite activity: You're not hanging around for a second helping of the chore. So, my friends decided to head off to a favorite watering hole and left instructions where I was to meet them when I finished my assigned task. Once again, I washed that car, this time with particular attention to every square inch of surface, double- and triple-checking my work. I asked my dad to come and inspect it, hoping that this time there would be no excuse to prevent me from leaving, but he outfoxed me by opening the doors and finding imperfections in the job from within. He walked away, once again telling me I wasn't finished and put me on restriction for the rest of the day.

At that time, I thought my dad was the biggest SOB on the planet, and as someone who has served as father to three of my own children, I can still sympathize with that young boy. I taught my own children the same kinds of lessons, but I did so gently. Then again, I wasn't gone from the scene for six months on end with nothing but hope that my children would make good choices and turn out all right. Over time, I came to realize that my dad was bestowing upon me a "Boy Named Sue" lesson designed to stay with me throughout my life. Thereafter, I was always obsessed with doing a thorough job and paying close attention to detail.

"A Boy Named Sue" is a famous Johnny Cash song in which the narrator relates how his father named him Sue and then left the family. Growing up, he hates the SOB who stuck him with a girl's name that embroils him in fights his whole life. As an adult, he meets his father in a bar and engages him in a knock-down, drag-out barnyard brawl that leaves teeth, blood, and skin all over the bar floor. When Sue demands an explanation for ruining his life by saddling him with that name, his father offers him a new perspective: The fight he has just seen in his son is proof that he did the right thing:

> **BUT YOU OUGHT TO THANK ME, BEFORE I DIE**
> **FOR THE GRAVEL IN YOUR GUTS AND THE SPIT IN YOUR EYE**
> **BECAUSE I'M THE SON-OF-A-BITCH THAT NAMED YOU SUE.[10]**

The narrator drops his gun, unfurls his fist, throws his arms around his pa, and promises that if he has a son, he's going to name him … Bill or George or anything but Sue!

Looking back nearly sixty years, I better understand what my dad was up to—and I thank him for the gravel in my guts and the spit in my eye, not for brawling, which I've never done, but for refusing to settle for second best because only the guy in first gets the gold medal. My father and I were never close, in part because he was absent for half my childhood and in part because I disappointed him so by quitting school, avoiding the military, and taking the journey in life that I took. He wanted that to be just so, too, and since I forged my own path, one scary and unfamiliar to him, he could never wrap his mind around it and acknowledge that it had worked for me, even if it might not be the best choice for most men's sons. A hardheaded navy man, he had a tough time admitting that it had worked out well for me and that I was a credit to the

10 Johnny Cash, vocalist, "A Boy Named Sue," by Shel Silverstein, track 56 on The Essential Johnny Cash, accessed December 18, 2024, https://genius.com/Johnny-cash-a-boy-named-sue-lyrics.

family, a good person who was earning much more than he ever made at a very young age. That said, I knew he must have secretly husbanded some pride late in his own life when he saw the company I founded survive, then succeed, then thrive. And I knew he heard the reviews from people who owned Scout Boats and praised the beauty, performance, reliability, and special features. At some point unacknowledged, I knew my father must have thought to himself, *That stupid kid has done okay for himself and for my daughter-in-law and grandchildren.*

My father lived into his nineties, and we started to become closer in his waning years. I escorted him on a tour of the factory and took him out for wonderful days of leisure on our own boat and told him about the achievements of his grandkids in the company and even about how one of his great-grandchildren had begun working with us. In 2023, a few months before he died, I was helping take care of him, and he uttered the words I had given up hearing but that meant the world to me:

"I'm proud of you."

I'm tearing up as I write this because other than Dianne saying yes, I can't think of any words that any person ever said to me that opened the floodgates to such unbridled relief, joy, and happiness as those four. I have been blessed in my life to hear a lot of great words—like "It's a healthy boy (or girl)" three times, or "I would like to buy that boat" thousands of times, or "Congratulations, you've been elected to the Hall of Fame"—but none were as long a time coming or as hard fought to earn as my dad's. That acknowledgment from my father was validation of everything I've ever achieved in my life. He was not proud of me simply for building a profitable $150 million company but for everything one could consider an achievement: developing a skill building something; learning to manage other people, including some a generation older than I was; starting, growing, and managing a successful company; marrying my life partner and raising three great kids; befriending a gaggle of amazing, smart, accomplished, good-hearted people; seeing much of this planet; and probably most significantly, developing a set of values for life and business and infusing them into my family, my company and all its employees, and every other aspect of my life.

Spanning the globe has reinforced my deeply held belief that anyone from anywhere in our benighted country, no matter the circumstances of their birth or the forces arrayed against them, can, with good health, rise to a life of great fortune. The tried-and-true formula involves treating oneself and others with respect, being honest and delivering on promises, remaining humble, working hard and maintaining the highest standards, never giving up, choosing gratitude for every blessing, remaining a student every day of life, and consorting with quality individuals. It is a formula that took me—a shy middle child with little formal education—to unfathomable heights, and it can do the same for almost anyone else. That is what my dad was validating, at least that is how I'm choosing to interpret it, and that is what I believe is involved in being a Boat Boy.

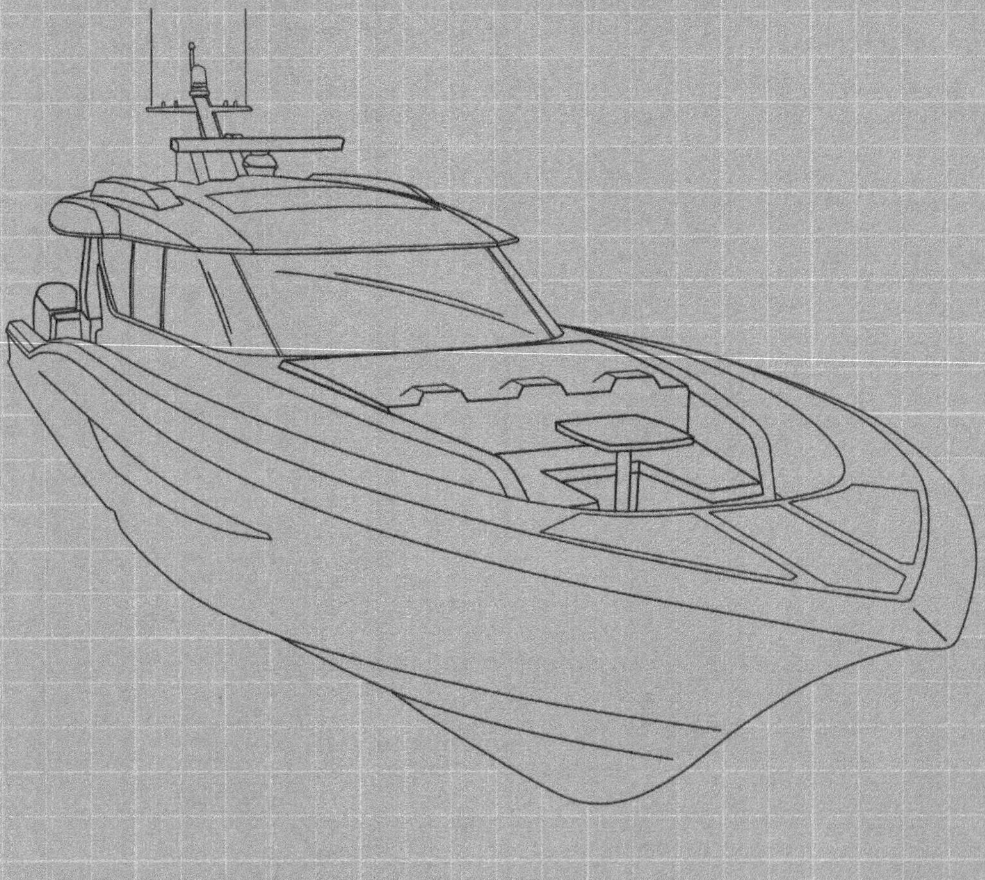

GALLERY

145 Sportfish being lifted onto yacht to be used as a tender

25-year anniversary of Scout Boats—employee group photo in 2014

Scout Factory, Plant A

One of the first 14-foot Scouts that Steve and Dianne built

Steve driving a 15-foot Scout

Steve driving a 14-foot Scout

Steve and Stevie driving a 14-foot Scout

Steve working in the original factory, clamping a hull and deck together

The original factory that was destroyed by Hurricane Hugo. Out front, the truck and trailer Steve used to travel and sell his boats.

Steve in the original factory, cleaning up late at night

Hurricane damage to the original factory

10,000th boat

New temporary factory near Jedburg airport after storm damage, before moving to current location

Current location, before many expansions. This shows plants A and B and the refurbish shop. We now have four more buildings.

Steve driving a 15-foot Scout

Building a 17-foot center console and dual console in production

172 Dorado with twin Honda motors

First boat display in the Atlanta boat show

Engineering team reviewing plans for a new model

Miami Boat Show—original Scout that Steve built at the outboard shop in front, 350 Abaco in the back

Steve at the plant

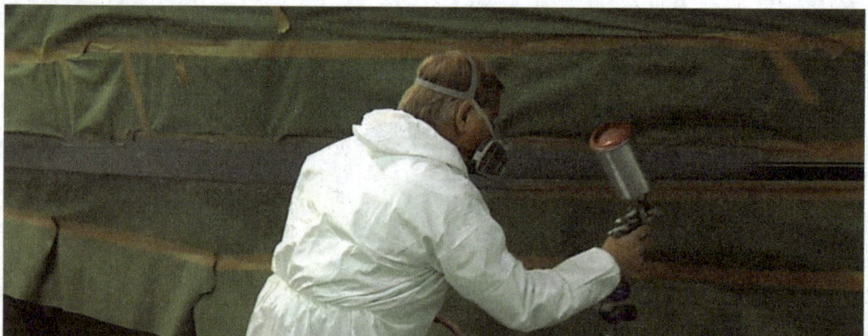

Steve spraying an accent stripe on the side of a boat